Weekends *for* Two

2nd Edition

Special Places to Stay
Romantic Restaurants to Visit
A Variety of Things to Do and See

In Virginia, West Virginia, Pennsylvania, Maryland, Delaware,
New Jersey, and Washington, D.C.

by: June Harrington Marquis
illustrations: Lisa Ann Marquis

Published by:
Liberty Publishing Company, Inc.
440 South Federal Highway
Deerfield Beach, Florida 33441

Library of Congress #84-80984
ISBN 0-89709-177-9

Cover photo:
David M. Barron/Oxygen Group

Manufactured USA

TABLE OF CONTENTS

INTRODUCTION

Are you spending your weekends doing the grocery shopping, cleaning the house, mowing the yard, or going to the kids' soccer games? How many times have you said, "We need to get away!" Often, deciding where to go, finding a good place to stay, and walking the streets looking for a great restaurant make it all seem more trouble than it's worth. *Weekends for Two* plans complete weekends for you with a wide range of places and many options.

 • Country inns—although many are included, along with sophisticated urban hotels, ski resorts and lakeside condos.

 • Restaurants—although many are described in each section and there is a restaurant index in the back.

 • Sightseeing—although information on things to do and see at each place is included.

 • Family trips—although some of the places mentioned might be suitable for bringing along the children.

Included in *Weekends for Two* is a variety of destinations: big cities with spectacular hotels, mountain lodges with panoramic views, lakeside condos with boating at the door, and small country inns offering breakfast in bed. The criteria for inclusion are a place to stay with a very special atmosphere, good food available, and some nearby interesting activity—ranging from historical sightseeing to a simple walk through the woods to a peaceful lake. Information on over 100 restaurants is also included.

A getaway weekend for two in a romantic setting can have the effect of a real vacation. We are fortunate to have so many varied and excellent places that are easily accessible. Take advantage of it! It's time to "stop and smell the flowers!" Choose your direction, make your reservations, toss a few clothes into a suitcase, and be on your way!

HOW TO USE THIS BOOK

The book is divided into five sections: Heading North, Heading South, Heading West, Heading East, and Heading for the Capitol, with Washington, D.C. as the center. These are more intuitive directions than geographical. There are destinations for those in need of just a quiet place to be alone together and places with lots of action—boating, shopping, sightseeing, and sports.

All of the places to stay are special, thus requiring reservations. In the larger cities, reservations for some of the restaurants may also be necessary. While there are no prices listed, as they can quickly become outdated, each place to stay has been loosely categorized as "very reasonable," "moderate," or "expensive but worth it." Call or write for current information—addresses and telephone numbers are included. For all large hotels, ask about their special weekend plans.

The book assumes that your getaway weekend for two begins on Saturday morning and ends Sunday afternoon. For places such as Prospect Hill, Wayside Inn, or the Inn at Buckeystown, which are somewhat isolated, this will probably be the right amount of time. For places such as Atlantic City, Philadelphia, and the Pennsylvania Dutch country, which offer a variety of sights and activities, it might be better to begin your weekend on Friday.

If you know of other good places that fit the criteria mentioned in the Introduction, please send the information to me in care of the publisher for consideration in a future edition.

N

- 7-Springs Lodge
  Champion

- Will O' Wisp
  Deep Creek

- The Hotel Hershey
  Hershey

- The Inn at Phillips Mill
  New Hope

Historic
Strasburg Inn •
Strasburg

- The Warwick
  Philadelphia

- Hotel duPont
  Wilmington

- Bavarian Inn
  Shepherdstown
  - Inn at Buckeystown
    Buckeystown

Harrah's Marina •
Atlantic City

- Mainstay Inn
  Cape May

- L'Auberge Provencale
  White Post

- Maryland Inn
  Annapolis

Red Fox Inn •
Middleburg

- Vista International
  Washington, D.C.

- Wayside Inn
  Middletown

- Crystal Gateway
  Arlington

- The Inn at Narrow Passage
  Woodstock

- Kemp House Inn
  St. Michaels

- Conyers House
  Sperryville

- Skyland Lodge
  Skyline Drive

- Channel Bass Inn •
  Chincoteague

- Prospect Hill
  Trevillians

- Boar's Head Inn
  Charlottesville

- Williamsburg Inn
  Williamsburg

- Mountain Lake Resort
  Mountain Lake

not to scale

HEADING

NORTH.....

The Warwick Hotel
Philadelphia, Pennsylvania

For an intimate, elegant, English Renaissance style hotel in the middle of a large city, you don't have to go to London. Take the train to Philadelphia and stay at The Warwick. Originally opened in 1926, it has recently been completely refurbished and remains a luxurious classic in the tradition of fine hotels. A Philadelphia landmark, The Warwick prides itself on providing whatever you need to make your stay enjoyable, from liveried doormen to custom embossed, handmilled soap. Complimentary in-room movies, convenience shops and fashionable boutiques in the lobby level, and large, beautifully decorated guest rooms contribute to the enjoyment of your stay. The Warwick is ideally situated in the heart of Philadelphia's Rittenhouse Square area, just minutes from the theater, fine dining, and a variety of shopping opportunities.

The best advice is: take the train! If you haven't tried it recently, this is a great way to travel whenever possible and Philadelphia is the ideal destination for a ride on Amtrak. Amtrak has a special weekend fare of about $35 round trip. The ease and enjoyment of this type of travel make it well worth the price. The train arrives at the 30th Street Station, which is about two miles from The Warwick.

Arriving around noon, you may want to head for the South Street area of the city. Located right next to the Delaware river, this area has been restored, renovated and improved upon continually over the past ten years. The cobble-stoned Head House Square, former site of open-air produce markets, boarders on Newmarket with its varied collection of shops and restaurants. In the summertime there are jugglers, musicians and craftsmen to entertain the frequent visitors that this area of the city draws.

Just around the corner is South Street. Walk up and down this street and find the latest in popular fashion, eccentric boutiques, and Philadelphia antiques side-by-side. No visit to South Street is complete without a stop at Jim's Steaks; located on Fourth and South, here you will discover the famous cheesesteak that Philadelphians love.

For those who are more interested in history, head for either the Tourist Center at the Philadelphia Convention and Visitors Bureau, 1525 John F. Kennedy Boulevard or the Visitors' Center at Third and Chestnut. Guided bus tours are available to take visitors through the historical areas. At the Center, you can pick up the Visitors' Guide Map to Philadelphia as well as a guide for the two-mile Liberty Trail walk. The walk begins and ends at Independence Hall and passes twenty-five historic sites in the heart of Philadelphia including the Betsy Ross House, Christ Church (erected in 1727, it is where Washington, Adams, Franklin, Lafayette and many members of the Continental Congress worshipped), and the Old Custom House housing an exhibit of old Philadelphia furnishings and a portrait gallery of Revolutionary War patriots.

Philadelphia has many fascinating museums as well as historical sites. The Philadelphia Museum of Art is one of the finest galleries in the world and is right down Benjamin Franklin Parkway from the Rodin Museum, which houses the largest collection of Rodin's works outside of Paris. Along the same street is the Franklin Institute which should not be missed. It is an interactive science museum where everyone enjoys participating as well as learning from the exhibits.

The choices of where to go to dinner in Philadelphia are endless. For casually sophisticated Italian food, try Fratelli near Rittenhouse Square. Fratelli has a well-deserved reputation for enjoyable atmosphere, great food, and reasonable prices. One of the loveliest dining spots in the city is the walled, tree-shaded restaurant called The Garden. Depending on the weather, patrons may dine in the garden, on the covered deck, or in one of the dining rooms in the old townhouse. The menu is imaginative and the food is exceptional, although the prices are somewhat high. Reservations are a must, especially if you want to eat in the garden.

Two of the most famous restaurants in the city are both called Bookbinders. The original Bookbinders, located near the dockside of the Delaware River, opened just after the end of the Civil War. The newer Bookbinders is located in the center of the city, right near the Warwick Hotel. Both offer seafood dishes to nearly two thousand patrons a day. Many people feel as though a visit to Philadelphia is not complete without dining at one of the two Bookbinders.

One of the best—and most expensive—French restaurants in America is LeBec-Fin on Walnut Street. The elegant, intimate dining room seats just thirty. There are two seatings a night, at six and nine, with a fixed-price menu for six courses including dessert. Reservations are essential and should be made several weeks in advance for weekends.

Not to be missed is the Italian Market section in South Philly on Ninth Street between Wharton and Christian. This area of tiny row houses, many of them baroque palaces inside, is "Rocky" territory and allows the visitor to experience the real ethnic neighborhood. It is five blocks of honking traffic, screaming vegetable vendors, pasta and mozzarella cheese makers, and brawny bakers displaying their wares. The sidewalks are filled with tables of household goods; paintings of Stallone and other stars on black velvet adorn the stores and restaurants, and butchers offering everything from homemade raviolis to pig snouts dot the neighborhood. Two of the world-famous Philadelphia cheese-steak establishments are at the southern end of the area, Pat's King of Steaks and Geno's Ace of Steaks. For good Southern Italian cooking, try Villa DiRoma, Ralph's or Plumbo's Nostalgia farther up Ninth Street.

Other possibilities are The Knave of Hearts on South Street, a small, inexpensive quaint French retaurant; Apropos on Broad Street near City Hall, a casually sophisticated art-deco establishment with an innovative menu; and Cafe Nola on South Street for New Orleans cuisine and lots of atmosphere. In the "Old City" section, at 312 Race Street, is DiNardos, a non-nonsense, "old-neighborhood, wear-your-jeans" type restaurant serving great seafood and specializing in steamed crabs.

You may want to end your evening at The Warwick's Polo Bay, a disco that lets you talk. Or, for something different, take a cab to the Triangle Tavern at 10th and Reed. Referred to as the "living museum" of South Philadelphia, there is a lot of drinking, a lot of noise, and a show with a polka band. Also, the Borgia Cafe on Head House Square offers live jazz in a European-style setting.

To Get There: By Train! Take a cab from the 30th Street Station to the hotel.

For Reservations: Call 215-735-6000 or write The Warwick, 17th and Locust Streets, Philadelphia, Pennsylvania 19103. Moderate with the special weekend rate.

The Inn at Buckeystown
Buckeystown, Maryland

The Inn at Buckeystown is an elegant 1890's restored Victorian mansion. There are five beautifully decorated bedrooms which share three baths. The third floor is currently being renovated and will soon offer four more bedrooms and two baths. The public rooms, as well as a few of the sleeping rooms, have chandeliers and working fireplaces. All of the rooms have lovely period pieces and impressive Oriental rugs, and are impeccably clean.

Guests arrive at Buckeystown by driving several miles south of Frederick along country roads edged with farmlands before the distant hills. Buckeystown is a nationally registered historic village with pre-revolutionary roots and a strong Civil War influence. The village is on the Monocacy River and surrounded by Civil War sites, monuments, and markers. Colonial and Victorian homes line the streets and dot the area farmlands. The village boasts a well-known potter, Nancy Bodmer, of "The Stone House," and a large antique co-op, Buckey's Antiques.

Rates at the Inn include a four-course dinner with wine and a full breakfast, both served in a lovely dining room with china, crystal, and silver. Complimentary port wine is offered in the public rooms or on the wrap-around veranda.

After strolling down the main (and only) street of Buckeystown, you may want to motor north four miles to the city of Frederick. The town was founded in 1745. There are self-guided walking tours, cycling tours, and driving tours all described on detailed maps offered by the Tourism Council. All of Frederick County is an ideal setting for a relaxed getaway. It is nestled in the scenic Catoctin Mountain region where meandering country roads entice the visitor to explore the historic and picturesque countryside and communities.

A little farther north along Route 40 is Hagerstown with its Saturday morning farmer's market, pre-World War I style houses, an Izod outlet, and a Class A Baltimore Orioles farm team (something for everyone). The market, on West Church Street, is open on Saturday mornings from 6 to 11. In the Terrace section of town are several streets of Georgian, Spanish and Tudor Revival style houses; along South Prospect Street are large 19th- and 20th-century houses on a hill overlooking the historic downtown area. Apparel for men, women and children is sold at 40 to 60 percent discount at Fashion Flair, the Izod Outlet. From mid-April through the end of August, the Hagerstown Suns play at 7:30 on Saturday nights at the Memorial Stadium.

For an informal dinner in Hagerstown, head for Chic's Seafood on Summit Avenue and feast on steamed crabs and other well-prepared fresh seafood. For an unusual dessert the Krump family donut shop, in an alley between Spruce and Market streets sells hot donuts smelling of yeast and sugar to the public from 7 p.m. till 3 a.m.

Across the Potomac River, where it meets the Shenandoah, is Harper's Ferry National Historical Park. The best place to begin your visit is at the Visitor Center, which is open all year except Christmas and New Year's Day. At the Center are exhibits, introductory slide programs, and information on self-guided and conducted walks in the park.

Most of the activities in the park are centered around the summer months when employees in uniform or period clothing explain the significance of the town. Shopkeepers, businessmen, and townspeople are all dressed in costume and provide demonstrations of crafts and explanations of exhibits.

There is an excellent and easy hike up from the town which takes you to Jefferson Rock for a magnificent view of the converging of two rivers. The walk continues past the old Harper Cemetery and over to Fillmore Street past three historic houses. The park, which covers hundreds of acres of paths and woodlands, is a marvelous place for just wandering and picnicking. (For other interesting sites in the area, see The Bavarian Inn in the Index.)

If you return to Washington via Rt. 70, you may wish to exit at Rt. 109 to Comus and hike up Sugarloaf Mountain. This is really more a beautiful walk than a hike. When you reach the top, you will be delighted to see the spectacular view of the surrounding mountains and valleys. There are two walking paths leading from the parking lot to the mountain top; one is a gently sloping trail with benches, and the other is really stairs made of rocks. The panoramic view from the top affords you the opportunity of seeing Bull Run to the south, Catoctin and the Blue Ridge Mountains to the west, and the Frederick valley to the north.

To Get There: Take Route 270 west from the Washington Beltway. Go south on Route 85 to Buckeystown.

For Reservations: Call 301-874-5755, or write at 3521 Buckeystown Pike, Buckeystown, MD 21717. Very reasonable.

The Bavarian Inn
Shepherdstown, West Virginia

A weekend at the Bavarian Inn is perfect. High on a hill overlooking the Potomac River as it carves its way through the Blue Ridge Mountains, the accommodations couldn't be better. The food in the Inn is excellent, the Bavarian ambience inviting, and there are good walks as well as sightseeing nearby.

The restaurant and rathskeller are in the big stone house at the top of the hill; the guest rooms are in three recently built chalets a short way down the grassy slope toward the river. Accommodations are in the German motif and include four-postered, canopied beds. Some rooms have fireplaces and sunken whirlpool baths.

You may choose to spend the afternoon sitting on your balcony viewing the river and background mountains and watching the trains occasionally cross the bridge joining Maryland and West Virginia. There is a pool on the grounds and a delightful patio for lunch or dessert, all with the same marvelous views.

Nearby is the Antietam National Battlefield in Sharpsburg. This is an excellent place to bicycle around or you may want to motor through the eight-mile, self-guided tour. The Visitor's Center and Museum is a good place to start the tour. Along the way is the Burnside Bridge over Antietam Creek, a famous example of one of the bridges built by 19th century immigrants. The battle of Antietam, in 1862, not only altered the course of the Civil War but gave Abraham Lincoln the opportunity to issue the Emancipation Proclamation.

Shepherdstown is the oldest municipality in West Virginia. Driving in any direction to or from the town, you will see beautiful old houses, acres of farmlands, hills, and surrounding mountains in the distance. Don't hesitate to stop at one of the many country stores. Shepherd College, built in 1871, is located directly across from the Bavarian Inn. If you have not been to Harpers Ferry, a short distance away, see the Index for possibilities there.

Back at the Inn, a drink on the patio is in order in the warmer months; in the colder weather, head for the Rathskeller in the basement. Live entertainment is often featured.

The Bavarian Inn has been an award-winning restaurant for many years, only recently adding overnight accommodations. With the huge stone fireplace, German paintings, and glass wall overlooking the river, it will be difficult to find a better place to dine. The German-American cuisine features trout freshly caught from the mountain streams, beef rouladen, wiener schnitzel, sauerbraten, and knockwurst with sauerkraut. Alternatively, there is the Old South Mountain Inn in nearby Boonsboro, Maryland, known for its well-stocked wine celler, or the Cozy Inn in Thurmont, Maryland, featuring southern cooking.

A short distance south of Shepherdstown is the Charles Town Turf Club with famous thoroughbred racing from mid-September through mid-December. Operating since 1933, the Club has a modern Skyline Terrace dining room with trackside tables, an air-conditioned clubhouse, a grandstand cafeteria, and several pubs. The Charles Town races are exciting even if you choose not to bet—which is more complicated than you might think.

After a hearty German breakfast, you might consider white-water rafting. The Shenandoah River, as it merges with the Potomac at Harpers Ferry, is the perfect introduction to the excitement and beauty of white-water rafting. Qualified guides lead your trip through flat water, several ledges, and a series of mild rapids. The trip takes from three to five hours, depending on water level. Lunch is provided. For a unique view of Harpers Ferry and the Potomac Water Gap, take a Potomac boat trip in the morning or evening down the river to the mountain bird sanctuary. A satisfying breakfast or supper is cooked over an open fire and served at the end of the trip. For information on either of these, contact River and Trail Outfitters, Inc., Box 246, Valley Road, Knoxville, Maryland, or Blueridge Outfitters at 304-725-3444.

To Get There: Take Rt. 270 from the Washington Beltway west to Frederick, head north on Rt. 40 to Boonsboro, take Rt. 34 to Shepherdstown.

For Reservations: Call 304-876-2551 or write Rt. 1, Box 30, Shepherdstown, WVA 25443. Moderate to Expensive.

Seven Springs
Champion, Pennsylvania

Seven Springs has it all. Known primarily as a ski resort, the facilities and activities are so extensive, summer or winter, skier or non-skier, that there is plenty to do. This is your one-stop getaway weekend for two.

Located in the Pennsylvania mountains, about an hour east of Pittsburgh, Seven Springs was originally an Alpine-type lodge constructed of logs with large, blazing fireplaces. Today it includes a highrise condo-type addition, an indoor swimming pool, saunas, hot tubs in the snow, indoor miniature golf, bowling, rollerskating, game rooms, outdoor tennis courts, and hiking trails. Has anything been left out? In the winter, there are ski slopes of varying difficulties with multiple chair lifts as well as cross country ski trails through the woods.

The types of accommodations are varied and include main lodge rooms with excellent views of the ski slopes and private balconies, family-type rooms (two bedrooms sharing a bath) in the highrise, cabins in the woods, and townhouse style condominiums.

Particularly in the winter season, a wise choice is a lodge room facing the slopes. Watching the skiers come down the mountainside as you sit on your balcony in the sun or in your warm room in front of the picture windows is one of the nicest features of Seven Springs. The slopes are lighted at night to extend your viewing time.

There are several places to eat at the Resort. The main dining room usually has a spectacular buffet complete with ice carvings and a dessert table. A smaller dining room with ala carte ordering from a menu, features steaks, chicken, and ribs. A coffee shop with sandwiches, soups, and desserts, and a fast-food hamburger and fried chicken shop complete the offerings in the main lodge. Out in the ski rental area, there are several large cafeterias with donuts, chili, sandwiches, soups, and hot chocolate as well as an outdoor facility offering knockwursts and hamburgers cooked over an open fire. Back in the woods is a charming gourmet French restaurant. The candlelight, crackling fires, soft music, and attentive service offer everything needed to complete a really memorable meal.

In the main lodge are boutiques and gift shops, several lounges serving "gluwein" in the winter as well as other liquors, beer and wine, and often offering entertainment and dancing. In other rooms, there may be bingo one night, a skiing movie another, or even a square dance.

While the skiing is perhaps as extensive as any place in the area, this can also be an excellent weekend away for non-skiers in winter or any season.

To Get There: Take Rt. 270 west to Frederick and head
  north on Rt. 70 to the Pennsylvania Turnpike. Head west
  on the Turnpike, getting off at Somerset. From Somerset,

go north to Champion. There are many Seven Springs signs along the way.

For Reservations: Call 814-352-7777 or write Seven Springs, Champion, Pa. 15622. Moderate.

Will O' The Wisp
Condominiums
Deep Creek Lake, Maryland

Will O' The Wisp Condominiums have recently been
built on Maryland's largest lake—Deep Creek Lake in Garrett County. An eight-story, gracefully modern mid-rise,
the project contains forty-seven apartments, each with an
uncluttered, sweeping view of the lake. In the resort are
such facilities as an indoor pool and sauna, an exercise
room, a good restaurant, and often live entertainment in
the lounge.

Each apartment has large sliding glass doors and windows overlooking Deep Creek Lake, a lakeside balcony or

patio, and a fireplace. The accommodations are equipped with air conditioning, automatic electric heat, and color television, and are well furnished with kitchen equipment, bedding, and linens.

A 700-foot gradually sloping sandy beach, boat docks and a protected swimming area are just a few steps from your apartment. Boats are available for rent including canoes, pontoon boats, sailboats, and water bikes. Sailing and waterskiing lessons are also available and lake cruises are scheduled daily.

Deep Creek Lake covers six square miles and offers over sixty-five miles of shoreline. Waterskiing, fishing, and sailing are very popular. Many individually-owned cottages line the lakefront. Nearby is the Wisp ski area, the largest ski area in Maryland, with an elevation of 3080 feet. There is a variety of lifts, twelve miles of runs and picturesque trails, a ski lodge housing a cafeteria, a ski rental shop, and clothing and equipment shops. During the off season, visitors may take the lift to the top of the mountain for a 12-mile panoramic view.

Two other places to visit in the area are the Appalachian Shop on Deep Creek Drive—an outlet for more than seven hundred mountain craftsmen—and Herrington Manor State Park located in Swallow Falls State Forest. Abundant wildlife, beautiful wildflowers and a variety of birds make this park ideal for nature study and long walks through the woods.

Artistic productions of high professional caliber can be found during the summer months at the Garrett County Playhouse on the Lake. Now in its twenty-fifth season, the Playhouse is located at the Blue Barn. All productions are under the direction of Dr. Yell, Professor of Drama at the University of New Mexico. This is one of the few stock theaters still operating in the United States. It is a theater-in-the-round and produces a different play each week during the season.

If fixing a dinner for two in your own condo, dining in front of your fireplace or on your balcony overlooking the lake doesn't appeal to you, there are several alternatives.

At the Resort, the Bavarian Room with its old world atmosphere provides excellent informal dining. Features of the house are the elaborate salad wagon, cheese table, and hot soup pot, from which you may help yourself. The fireplace helps make your wine or favorite cocktail even more enjoyable in cold weather. The Four Seasons Dining Room is adjacent to the condominiums for continental cuisine in an elegantly appointed cathedral-ceilinged room overlooking the lake.

Nearby are two other restaurants offering lakefront views. The Red Run Inn is situated in a serene setting of forests and trails and offers a large salad bar and a menu ranging from fresh seafood to prime rib. Upstairs in the same building is the Crab Galley, featuring steamed crabs and seafood delicacies along with soup and sandwiches.

The Silver Tree, adjacent to Alpine Village, specializes in Italian food but also offers seafood, chicken, and other dishes. In the winter season, the working fireplaces lend additional charm to the restaurant. Live entertainment is featured on the weekends.

To Get There: Take the Washington Beltway to Route 270 and head west towards Frederick. From Frederick, take Rt. 70 through Hagerstown to Hancock. Take Rt. 40 west to Cumberland, Rt. 48 west to Keysers Ridge, and Rt. 219 south to Deep Creek Lake.

For Reservations: Call 301-387-5503 or write Will O'The Wisp, Rt. 219, Oakland, Maryland 21550. Very reasonable.

Hotel duPont
Wilmington, Delaware

The Hotel duPont is located in the heart of downtown Wilmington, Delaware. Built in 1913, this spacious and elegant hotel provides a delightful retreat to an old world style of courtesy and accommodations. The two hundred and ninety guest rooms and suites are beautifully furnished and individually decorated with all desired hotel amenities. Although rates during the week are very high, weekend rates are half-price.

Many shops are located in the Hotel including a beauty salon, barber shop, travel agency, and clothing boutiques. A short distance from the Hotel is the Market Street Mall, a pedestrian mall with restored historic buildings, sidewalk cafes and a variety of shops. On the mall is the Grand Opera House, one of the finest examples of cast iron architecture in the country. The 19th-century Victorian style building is in full use today hosting symphonies, concerts, dance, and operas, all bathed in a soft glow from the four immense etched-glass chandeliers.

Wilmington has been duPont country since Revoluntionary days when the duPonts, as French immigrant friends of Lafayette, moved from New Jersey to Delaware. One should not visit the area without planning an afternoon at the Winterthur Museum and Gardens. Located a short distance northwest of Wilmington on Route 52, Winterthur was the country estate of H. F. duPont. During his lifetime (1890-1969), it was a self-contained, nearly self-sustaining community, complete with turkey and sheep farms, vegetable gardens, greenhouses, golf course, saw mill, railroad station, post office, and even a prize winning herd of Holstein cattle. H. F. duPont was one of America's eminent collectors of American antiques and today Winterthur houses more than 50,000 objects in a nine-story building on the estate that includes 200 landscaped acres, rolling meadows, and untouched woods. There are 196 rooms and display areas, a spectacular public garden like no other, and guided tours by open-air, motorized trams offered spring through autumn.

A little south of Winterthur on Route 52 is Hagley Museum depicting 19th-century American industry and life. Here is a marvelous place to wander through 200 acres along the scenic Brandywine River, the original site of the duPont black powder works. Explore restored mills, a worker's home, school house, stone quarry, and machine shops. Demonstrations of crafts and a French-style garden provide additional interests.

Just north of Wilmington is Nemours, the 300-acre country estate of Alfred I. duPont. Tours of the mansion and gardens begin with tea on the patio and proceed through the 102-room mansion where many of the rooms are furnished with fine examples of antique furniture, rare rugs, tapestries, family portraits, and outstanding works of art. Reservations for the two-hour tour are recommended and may be made by calling (302) 651-6912.

The Chadds Ford area, home of Longwood Gardens and the Brandywine River Museum, is a short distance north of Winterthur. At Kennett Square, Longwood Gardens is an incomparable indoor-outdoor horticultural display on a 350-acre country estate once belonging to Pierre duPont. It will take at least half of a day to see the gardens and conservatories; a terrace restaurant offers both full- and self-service dining. Close by is the Brandywine River Museum, an art museum in a century-old grist mill whose charm has been carefully preserved. The Museum's paintings hang in galleries of handhewn beams, pine floors, and white plastered walls—a striking background for this excellent collection. There are works by Andrew Wyeth, his father (N. C. Wyeth), his son James, and other famous artists of the region including Howard Pyle, Maxfield Parrish, and Harvey Dunn.

In the Chadds Ford area there are many places to dine, including Longwood Inn featuring mushroom and Chesapeake seafood specialties; the Brandywine River Museum Restaurant, located in a glass tower overlooking the river and open for lunch only; Buckley's Tavern in Centreville, an historic village between Longwood Gardens and Winterthur; and the Chadds Ford Inn, an historic 18th-century stone inn and tavern decorated with Wyeth art.

The Hotel duPont offers two excellent choices for dining–the Green Room and the Brandywine-Christina Room. Dining in the Green Room is an experience in the tradition of European elegance—a setting of serene grandeur, impeccable service, and gourmet food. The Brandywine-Christina Room, with its handsome 18th-Century American decor, is more intimate but no less impressive with its collection of paintings by three generations of Wyeths. The Brandywine-Christina Room is noted for its fine beef, seafood dishes, and flaming desserts. The Green Room Lounge is a charming spot for a drink and offers a sumptuous Sunday brunch.

Alternatively, the Columbus Inn on Pennsylvania Avenue is an 18th-Century building with a Colonial, candlelit atmosphere. The menu is Continental, leaning toward French, generally excellent in execution, and moderately priced. Along the previously mentioned Market Street Mall are several small, cozy restaurants and sidewalk cafes.

To Get There: Take I-95 north to Exit 17 to Rt. 52 to the Hotel which is on the corner of Market Street.

For Reservations: Call 800-441-9019 or write the Hotel duPont, Box 991, Wilmington, Delaware 19899. Moderate with the special weekend rate.

The Historic Strasburg Inn
Strasburg, Pennsylvania

The Historic Strasburg Inn is set on fifty-eight acres amidst miles and miles of Pennylvania Dutch farmland. Somehow the Inn is able to combine the best of a country inn and a charming resort. The accommodations are excellent—authentically furnished in Pennsylvania Dutch style—and you may wish to spend your entire weekend strolling about the spacious grounds, bicycling over the numerous trails, splashing in the circular pool, and eating the delicious Pennsylvania Dutch food.

A little background . . . "Pennsylvania Dutch" is a cultural rather than a religious designation used to describe natives of Lancaster County and the surrounding area. The Amish are part of this Pennylvania Dutch group, which means they have a German ancestry while speaking the Pennsylvania Dutch dialect. Approximately 12,000 persons make up the Old Order Amish population of Lancaster County with another 12,000 members of the Mennonite Community residing there. These are the "plain people." These people typically pursue agricultural life styles, are identified with the use of horse-drawn buggies, have a distinctive style of dress, and strictly adhere to religious beliefs which prohibit electricity, telephones, and television in their homes.

Because most of the places you might want to visit are closed on Sundays, it is suggested you begin your weekend with sightseeing at Intercourse, Pennsylvania, and work your way down to Strasburg for your stay at The Inn. This is about a fifteen mile-drive.

Begin your visit to the Pennsylvania Dutch Country with a stop at The People's Place in Intercourse. Here is the Amish Story Museum featuring a three-screen documentary-"Who are the Amish," a movie on the Mennonites, a book and craft shop, and a courtyard art gallery.

An interesting place to stop while in Intercourse is Kitchen Kettle, a community of quaint shops each specializing in a particular item—flowers, jams, relishes, bakery goods, tobacco, smoked meats and cheeses, fudge, quilts, or pewter. At the craft shops, visitors can watch local girls sew bonnets, hand dip candles, and make ceramic pottery. Lunch is served at the Kettle House with a salad bar, good sandwiches, freshly baked pies, and homemade ice cream.

Heading west on Rt. 340 just outside of Intercourse, you will see the Plain & Fancy Farm. If you didn't lunch at the Kitchen Kettle, here is your first opportunity for family-style Pennsylvania Dutch food. Adjacent to the restaurant is a village of shops and museums including the Talbott Knitting Mills Factory Outlet, a gold and silver shop, and an Ice Cream Parlor. The Amish Barn, just a mile or two past Plain & Fancy, is a similar type restaurant with Pennsylvania Dutch atmosphere, some shops, and a bakery.

Continuing west about six miles from Intercourse is Bird-In-Hand. One of seven farmers' markets in the Lancaster area, the stands offer such items as homemade baked goods, seafood, mushrooms, health foods, freshly picked vegetables, Pennsylvania Dutch potato chips and pretzels, funnel cakes, and assorted candies. On the grounds are several factory outlets, including the Susquehanna Glass Co. with shelves and shelves of glass and dinnerware at discount prices.

About two miles farther west, turn left on Rt. 896. You are now headed in the direction of Strasburg. Before going to the Inn, you may want to take a short detour west on Rt. 30 and visit an Amish farm. There are three to choose from. About three miles west, at the red covered bridge, is the Amish Farm and House located on twenty-five acres of farmland, all with crops or animals. A hostess gives a guided lecture through the ten-room house explaining the plain people's way of life. About two miles farther is the Amish Homestead, a seventy-one acre farm (dating back to 1744) in full operation with horse-power and mule-power still utilized for plowing and harvesting. There are family gardens, a large variety of farm animals, and acres of growing crops, along with a guided tour through the house and farm buildings.

Going back to Rt. 896, heading south towards Strasburg, you have the opportunity to stop at The Amish Village, about two miles north of the Inn. Here, also, you can have a guided tour of an old Amish farmhouse, visit an authentically furnished one-room Amish schoolhouse, a blacksmith shop, a springhouse, an operating smoke house, and the Amish Village store. The famous Pennsylvania Dutch pretzels are baked here in the 200-year-old ovens.

Time to head for the Historic Strasburg Inn, rock lazily on the porch, or take a dip in the pool before dinner. Excellent dining is available at the Inn's Washington House. During the weekend, the Inn offers three special events in the fine tradition of Colonial feasting. On Friday night, there is a seafood feast with a raw seafood bar for appetizers, a salad table containing twenty different assorted salads, and an almost endless array of entrees including freshly steamed clambakes, rainbow trout, and shrimp scampi. A choice from the dessert table ends the menu.

On Saturday between 4:00 p.m. and 8:00 p.m. and on Sunday between 3:00 p.m. and 8:00 p.m., the Inn offers buffet dining. Hot chafing dish items such as roast beef, broasted chicken, sausage, and peak-of-the-season vegetables, along with salads, fruits, cheeses and freshly baked pies and cakes are available on an all-you-can-eat basis. Each evening, those who prefer may order ala carte and dine by candlelight in one of three beautifully decorated dining rooms.

On Sundays from 10 a.m. until 2 p.m., a Sunday brunch is served in the cordial mood of Early America. Hot chafing dish items, flavorful vegetables, fruits, cheeses, warm baked goods, and more desserts are served amidst shimmering ice carvings. Sunday brunch is hard to find in this area of the country as most establishments are not open on Sundays.

Before leaving the Pennsylvania Dutch Country, take the hour-long ride on America's oldest steam railroad through the picturesque Amish farmlands on wooden coaches dating from the turn of the century. This is the train that was featured in "Raintree Country" and several of the coaches were in the movie "Hello Dolly." The Strasburg Railroad operates year-round except from mid-December to mid-January and is located about three miles from the Inn.

To Get There: Take I-95 North; Go west on the Baltimore Beltway to Exit 24, north on Rt. 83 to York, east on Rt. 30 around Lancaster. About eight miles east of Lancaster, take Rt. 896 to Strasburg. Or, if you want to head directly to Intercourse, off Rt. 30, east of Lancaster, take Rt. 340 east to Intercourse.

For Reservations: Call 717-687-7691 or write the Historic Strasburg Inn, Rt. 896, Strasburg, Pennsylvania 17579. Moderate.

Hotel Hershey
Hershey, Pennsylvania

The Hotel Hershey advertises that it is the "only Four Star Resort in Pennsylvania." Situated high on a peaceful hill with a commanding view of the surrounding countryside and offering every resort amenity imaginable, guests soon come to understand why the Hotel has been awarded not only the Mobil four-star rating but four diamonds from AAA as well.

The colors and tiles of the Mediterranean welcome you in the beautiful fountain lobby where guests are often served wine and light appetizers before dinner. There are 270 tastefully appointed rooms and suites in the Hotel, some overlooking the grounds and others the indoor pool. All rates include either all three meals or just breakfast and dinner. The meals consist of several courses or a buffet of top quality, well-prepared food. The circular glass dining room overlooks the gardens and ponds; in line with the atmosphere of refined informality, men are required to wear coats and ties for dinner.

The Hotel Hershey offers several vacation and holiday packages. Among those of particular interest are the "Hershey Float Package," which includes a one-hour flight in a hot air balloon above the lush, rolling countryside; "Christmas in Hershey," which includes several festive holiday events and special foods and runs from mid-November to December 30th; and "Freedom Weekends," available in the off season at the lowest rates.

Three championship 18-hole golf courses and two beautiful 9-hole courses lead the activities available throughout the hotel grounds. The grounds also include tennis courts, horseback riding, lawn bowling, cross country skiing, bicycle and hiking paths, and year-round swimming. Adjacent to the indoor pool is a whirlpool and sauna. Other indoor opportunities include gift shops, exercise rooms, game rooms, a sandwich shop and the cozy Iberian Lounge and Bar featuring entertainment nightly.

Hershey Park is within walking distance of the Hotel. Even if you don't want to try the other forty thrilling rides, you might enjoy the panoramic view of the park from the relaxing Sky Ride. The park has several restaurants and entertainment ranging from Broadway-show performances to country music singers and Rock n' Roll groups playing music from the fifties. The park is open all of June, July, and August and during some weekends in May and September.

Close by is Hershey's Chocolate World Visitors Center. The free, animated tour of Hershey's candy from bean to bar is truly unforgettable and the aroma of chocolate cooking undeniable. Also not to be missed are the spectacular

Hershey Gardens in the same area. This is a 23-acre botanical oasis with vibrant displays in six theme gardens; rare trees and shrubs are interspersed with award-winning flower collections including some 35,000 roses.

The legend of Milton S. Hershey is a true story of success and philanthropy. He was a poor central Pennsylvania farm boy who became a self-made millionaire by building a chocolate empire in a cornfield. To get a feeling for the picture of Mr. Hershey's life, take the tour through the Milton Hershey School, the school he founded to provide a home and tuition-free education for 1200 children who are orphaned or deprived of a normal family life. Tours include a visit to Founders Hall, the monument to Mr. Hershey. Milton Hershey wanted a "real home town" and Hershey, Pennsylvania, is just that. With tree-lined streets, well-kept houses and beautifully manicured green areas, it is one of the most immaculate, well-planned towns in America.

The Hotel Hershey is a world of elegance, beauty and entertainment enhanced by warm and friendly Pennsylvania hospitality. Perhaps that's why it's been rated one of the very best resorts in North America.

To Get There: Take I-95 to Baltimore, then I-83 north. South of Harrisburg, PA, take 422 east and follow the signs to the Hotel Hershey.

For Reservations: Call 1-800-533-3131 or write The Hotel Hershey, P.O. Box BB, Hershey, Pennsylvania 17033. Moderate with the inclusion of the meals.

The Inn at Phillips Mill
New Hope, Pennsylvania

One could hardly imagine a more intimate and romantic country getaway than the Inn at Phillips Mill. Clustered beneath towering shade trees on either side of a sharp bend in the road, the stone buildings, courtyards, and the old mill are from bygone days. The mill is no longer in operation but its buildings have been put to good use; they house a first class country-style French restaurant and five sets of guest quarters romantically appointed in the country tradition. The surrounding farms sloping to the Delaware River add little to remind you of the encroachment of the modern world. Yet, you are only a couple of minutes from downtown New Hope with all its charm and attractions.

The guest quarters, some of which include sitting rooms and stone fireplaces, have been individually decorated with quilting, aprons, cushions, four-poster beds, and antique rocking chairs. No two of the rustic rooms are alike, but if they look familiar it is because numerous advertisements in Better Homes and Gardens and other publications have been photographed here. The rooms are in great demand; it is necessary to make reservations far in advance.

The restaurant maintains an essentially French country cuisine, lightened and broadened by a touch of the nouvelle. The menu is a la carte, which can run up the bill a bit, but this is balanced by a strictly bring your-own wine policy (the Inn does not hold a liquor license). The informality of the restaurant works well with the professional geniality of the staff and the country atmosphere. There are three different dining areas, all of them warm and comfortably rustic. You can have your meal around the fireplace in the upstairs den, downstairs in the cozy front room, or on the terra cotta terrace overlooking the garden in the rear. During the summer months, the courtyard garden is also available for alfresco dining.

In keeping with its first class quality, the restaurant is not inexpensive; however, it is worth every penny you might pay for such delights as the chef's own tureen or mousse, fresh tomato consomme, maybe an endive or red lettuce and watercress salad dressed with tiny orange slices and nuts, followed perhaps by veal or salmon in a delicate sauce and garnished with a zucchini section stuffed with stewed tomato and basil. Do not overlook the desserts, all prepared in The Inn's kitchen. The restaurant does not accept credit cards but will take personal checks.

This is a marvelous region for long drives in the countryside. Quaint towns and villages, unusual shops, and an abundance of restaurants and inns are in every direction. New Hope is an artists' colony with many galleries, antique and specialty shops, and the well-known Bucks County Playhouse. The Golden Door Gallery, along the main street, is one of the largest art galleries in the Philadelphia area. Available here is original art work at prices below those in

Philadelphia-New York. The gallery is housed in a 200-year-old structure next to the Bucks County Playhouse. The building features brick floors, two-story ceilings, fieldstone walls, and a lounge area for browsing through art periodicals in front of a cozy fire. A special room dedicated to the work of Bucks County artists displays local scenes of Quaker fieldstone buildings, wooden canal bridges, and meandering streams.

New Hope offers a great many water-related activities. At Coryell's Ferry, behind Gerenser's Exotic Ice Cream Shop on Main Street, boat rides up the Delaware River operate every forty-five minutes in season. Mule barge trips on the historic Delaware Canal depart from The Barge Landing on New Street several times a day. At the Tow Path, you may rent bikes to ride along the canal, rent a canoe, take water skiing lessons, or try surf jetting on the river. Point Pleasant Canoes runs raft and canoe trips for beginners and tubing for the more adventuresome. Both of these trips offer lovely views of hills, trees, and covered bridges. If you prefer train transportation, try the fourteen-mile steam train ride through the beautiful Pennsylvania farmlands. The New Hope Railroad Station is an authentic railway post office car and has a fascinating gift shop.

Five miles south of New Hope along the Delaware River is Washington Crossing State Park, an internationally known historic site where Washington and his 2,400 men crossed the Delaware on Christmas night, 1776, to attack the Hessian troops. An impressive Memorial Building displays the only exact copy of the famous painting of this event, accompanied by narration and music. At the Park is Bowman's Hill State Wildflower Preserve, containing 800 species of wildflowers—the perfect place for a long walk in the spring and summer.

In addition to The Inn at Phillips Mill, the area has many fine restaurants. The Hotel DuVillage offers intimate country dining featuring country French cuisine. Nearby, Chez Odette has a similar fare. In good weather from the back room of Chez Odette or the open patio, guests have a beautiful view of the rippling Delaware River. A jazz trio is featured on the weekends.

A short distance north of New Hope, in Erwinna, is the Golden Pheasant, bordered by the Delaware River on one side and the Canal with swans on the other. Be sure to request a table in one of the three downstairs dining rooms. All are outstanding but different. Each area has a startlingly different personality; all are very pleasant; all share the same menu.

If you are planning to attend the Bucks County Playhouse, you may want to dine at the Playhouse Inn. Continental cuisine in a relaxed atmosphere is offered during the season in the old Inn overlooking the River.

Crossing the Delaware River into New Jersey and heading a few miles south you will come to The Inn at Sergeantsville. This tranquil village provides the atmosphere for elegant dining in its 18th-century stone structure. Exposed beams, pine floors, soft candlelight, peach flowered linens, original paintings, and piano music make the dining experience very special even before you enjoy the outstanding food. The chef takes advantage of seasonal specialties with a changing menu and specials every evening. Service is attentive without being obtrusive, the wine list is extensive, and each course is a presentation. A newly converted ice house offers cocktails or an after dinner drink.

If you make this a three-day weekend, you may want to enjoy the complimentary juice, coffee, and sweet rolls at The Inn at Phillips Mill one morning and head for Colligan's Stockton Inn across the river in New Jersey for brunch on Sunday. This inn was the setting for the Rodgers and Hart song "A Small Hotel with a Wishing Well" and has pleasant, old world charm with an excellent brunch served overlooking the river.

To get There: Take I-95 north to Route 32 west to New Hope. Continue on Rt. 32 north along the river for about three miles. The Inn is on the right.

For Reservations: Call 215-862-9911 or write at North River Road, New Hope, PA 18938. Moderate.

Harrah's Marina
Atlantic City, New Jersey

Close enough to the Boardwalk but far enough away
from the maddening crowds is Harrah's Marina Hotel, set
in a sea of rushes overlooking the Absecon Channel. The
hotel is plush and contemporary with a five-story atrium
greenhouse in the center of the lobby. The rooms are excep-
tionally clean, extravagantly decorated, and each has a
view of the water or the marshlands. The casino is subdued
and sophisticated with tuxedoed croupiers holding court.

This is a weekend that works best if you plan to spend
two nights. Harrah's has several package plans that include
breakfast, a show, and even a buffet dinner. The hotel is
located on eleven bayfront acres with their own baywalk.
A short walk takes you to the marina with a variety of

yachts and pleasure craft. Plenty of excitement is available at Harrah's with baccarat, roulette, craps, blackjack, and slots plus big-name headliners from the performance world. In addition, Harrah's offers deck tennis, a health club, a glass-enclosed pool, and five restaurants for casual to gourmet food without leaving the premises.

Arriving at noon, you will need to make a choice. Are you in the mood for an elegant luncheon in the Hotel's glass-walled French restaurant? Or are you ready to take a jitney out to the Boardwalk for one of those famous New Jersey hotdogs? Either way, you will probably eventually end up at the beach. A walk on the six-mile stretch of white sand by the crashing waves of the Atlantic is a great tonic for the urban dweller in any season. Jutting out from the Boardwalk are several piers. The Steel Pier offers stage shows, dancing, movies, and a giant ferris wheel; Garden Pier has concerts and an art gallery; Central Pier has a Sky Tower, giant slide and aquarium; Million Dollar Pier is a collection of seaside shops and restaurants.

Make the return trip along the Boardwalk, between the Golden Nugget and Resorts International. This strip of about three miles will give you an assortment of gypsy palm readers, handwriting analysts, saltwater taffy and fudge shops, oyster bars, art shops, fine jewelry shops, the towering, and shining reflective mirrors of the Atlantis facade, and the columns of Convention Hall.

Plan to get back in time for a drink in the atrium at Harrah's where a jazz band or string ensemble may be performing. Or visit the ice cream parlor in nearby Trump's Castle that overlooks the yachts and waterways.

The choices for dinner are varied. The Claridge Hotel, across a green lawn from the Boardwalk, has a glass-walled restaurant on the top floor with an excellent view of the ocean. The food is Continental, featuring many items fixed at your table. The Claridge Hotel itself provides a contrast to Harrah's. The tallest building in Atlantic City, it has a decidedly British ambiance. You are greeted by beefeaters and bobbies as you enter the quiet, wood-trimmed lobby.

The casino is the smallest in town and the atmosphere is intimate.

Alternatively, there is Capt. Starn's Seafood Restaurant located at the Inlet, seating 750 guests with three bars. This is a casual restaurant where you will enjoy lobster, crab, oysters and clams, caught by Capt. Starn's own fishing fleet, while overlooking the water and the boats.

Alfred's Villa on Pacific Avenue is easily reached by jitney or cab. Here are seven magnificently decorated dining rooms, each with a different theme. The menu is continental with an emphasis on seafood and steak. Try a bottle of "Gancia," a fine Italian sparkling burgundy not available in the Washington area.

After dinner, even if you are not a gambler, it is fun to walk through the various casinos. This is another world! In brief, the Golden Nugget is very Las Vegas styled, the walls mirrored in gold and croupiers dressed like riverboat gamblers. An enormous gilded cage houses large, electronically animated parrots who perform every quarter-hour providing imitations of famous Hollywood stars.

Next to Convention Hall is the Atlantis Hotel, with a tri-level casino overlooking the ocean and scantily clad waitresses serving drinks and a wide selection of food. At the other end of the Boardwalk is Resorts International Hotel. The casino is a huge, mirrored, red room with bells, flashing lights, and the clanking of money into slot machines. At all the casino/hotels, evening cabaret theaters offer dinner and Las Vegas-style shows, often with name stars.

Before breakfast the next morning, rent a bicycle; they are allowed on the Boardwalk until 9:00 a.m. Later, choose from a Sunday brunch offered in all the casino/hotels, a bagel on the Boardwalk, or hot rum buns in one of several sidewalk cafes. If you don't want to spend any more time in the casinos or on the beach, how about some boating? The previously mentioned Capt. Starn offers fishing boats, sightseeing cruises, sport fishing, and sailboats and speedboats for rent.

The city's skyline provides a spectacular view from on board the "Basin Queen" which departs from Gardner's

Basin three times a day. The "Flying Cloud" is a replica of a classic clipper ship and takes passengers for three-hour trips as well as serving alfresco dinner alongside the ship. While at the Basin, stroll around the restored fishermen's village, the aquarium, and other maritime exhibits.

To Get There: Take I-95 to the Walt Whitman Bridge, the North-South Freeway (Rt. 42) to the Atlantic City Expressway to Exit No. 9. Alternatively, a more leisurely route is via the car ferry at Lewes, Delaware (see Cape May) and up the Garden State Parkway directly into Atlantic City.

For Reservations: Call 609-441-5100 or write Harrah's Marina, 2700 Brigantine Blvd., Atlantic City, N.J. 08401. Moderate to expensive.

HEADING

SOUTH . . . . .

Prospect Hill
Trevillians, Virginia

Never heard of Trevillians, Virginia? Neither have most people. This, the special ambience of Prospect Hill, and gourmet dining make it the perfect place for a getaway weekend for two.

Located on a small country road fifteen miles east of Charlottesville, Prospect Hill is the home of Bill Sheehan, a former marketing representative for a large firm. Bill and his family have taken the 14-room main house, which dates back to the early 1700's, as well as several former slave cabins, and renovated them to make a very special inn in the Virginia countryside.

The rooms are well furnished, mostly in antiques, with a couch in front of the fireplace (where wood is stacked just waiting for you to light a fire), a small table with two chairs for your breakfast, and a large four-poster double bed. The slave quarters are suites with a bedroom, bath, and separate living room with fireplace and breakfast table.

Prospect Hill is situated on a small hill back in the trees and down a long driveway lined with two-hundred-year-old boxwoods. Plan your trip to arrive in the early afternoon in time to take a leisurely walk through the woods to the twenty-acre lake about a quarter of a mile from the house. When you return, you will be ready to enjoy the wine and fruit that was delivered to your room while you sit in front of your own crackling fireplace. You may watch dusk settle from the glider on the back porch of the main house as you look across the lawn shaded by enormous magnolia, tulip poplar, and beech trees.

An experience that is certainly unexpected in these "back hills" of Virginia is now at hand. Bill Sheehan is a gourmet cook. Several nights a week he prepares a five-course feast for his house guests and dinner guests from Charlottesville. It all takes place in the restored rooms of the main house. After sipping sherry in front of one of several fireplaces, you hear a dinner bell, indicating the meal is ready to be served. Guests are ushered into one of several small rooms with widely spaced tables beautifully set with linen, fresh flowers, silver, and candlelight. Bill describes what he has prepared for the evening and your feast begins. Homemade soup, salads and vegetables from the garden, freshly baked breads, delicious sauces on the exquisitely prepared entrees, and unusual desserts make Prospect Hill a special place to dine even if you are not staying overnight.

In the morning, at a reasonable hour, a houseboy will appear at your door with breakfast on a tray; most often it is french toast from the homemade bread baked for dinner, country sausage, freshly squeezed orange juice, and a large pot of coffee. You may have time for a morning fire before heading back through the hills of Virginia.

To Get There: Take Rt. 66 west and exit at Warrenton. From there take Rt. 29 to Culpepper, Rt. 15 south to Gordonsville, Rt. 33 east to Trevillians, and Rt. 613 south to Prospect Hill.

For Reservations: Call 703-967-0844, or write at Rt. 1, Box 65, Trevillians, VA 23170. Moderate with dinner and breakfast.

Mountain Lake Resort
Mountain Lake, Virginia

Do you feel the need for a weekend in the style of yesteryear? Perhaps a place on top of a mountain overlooking a lake, offering good food, simple pastimes such as scenic walks, paddle boats and carriage rides and almost guaranteeing serene, cool alpine days and refreshing evenings might be just what you're looking for. If so, Mountain Lake Resort is for you.

Located about twenty minutes from Blacksburg and Virginia Tech, Mountain Lake Resort lets you experience the type of vacation enjoyed in the south in earlier days, but with unobtrusive touches of contemporary living. The main lodge was built in 1937 of native stone and has been recently renovated. The lobby welcomes you with a spectacular stone fireplace, polished red-tiled floors and comfortable sofas and chairs, letting you know immediately you are in a true mountain lodge. Guest rooms are attractive. The suites include two-person whirlpool baths, and the rooms on the north side overlook the 69-acre lake. Accommodations are also available in white-frame cottages scattered at lakeside, and in the new Chestnut Lodge where rooms come with balconies and fireplaces. Upon arrival, if this looks vaguely familiar to you, it's because Mountain Lake Resort was the location for much of the filming of the movie "Dirty Dancing." In the movie, however, the Resort was depicted as a place in the Catskills; don't expect anything like the dancing and entertainment scenes.

Breakfast and dinner are part of the room rate; the quality and quantity of the food served makes this a real bargain. The large dining room is attractively decorated and the floor-to-ceiling windows look out over the lake and gardens. Dinner consists of several courses with choices in each course. The food is an interesting combination of southern cooking and continental cuisine, served by friendly, competent staff. A wine list is available. Breakfast gives you the choice of an elaborate buffet or ordering from the menu.

The Resort offers many leisuretime activities. Don't miss the hike around the lake and the one behind the main lodge leading to the mountain peak that lets you look across the valley to the mountains of West Virginia. Fishing for bass, horseback riding, swimming in the lake, horseshoes, croquet and even a clay tennis court are right at your door. Recently the Resort has remodeled an old barn; it now contains a large game room, television room, pub-type lounge yet retains the atmosphere of the mountain lodge with the exposed beams and stone fireplace. Connecting the main lodge with the recreation barn are several small shops, a weight room, a sauna and whirlpool baths. In the winter there are cross-country skiing with instruction and rentals, ice skating and horse-drawn sleigh rides.

Along I-81 on your way to or from Mountain Lake Resort, there is a lot to see and many dining opportunities worth a stop. For places to visit and eat at the northern end, where I-66 intersects with I-81, see the "Inn at Narrow Passage" section of this book. Staunton, a little farther south, is the birthplace of the nation's 28th President

Woodrow Wilson; tours of his home are offered daily and in the reception center are exhibits and a documentary film about the Wilson era. The Belleray Inn has good accommodations and food if you have some extra time—try their chocolate silk pie. Also in Staunton is the White Star Mill Restaurant, an ingeniously converted flour mill that serves excellent hearty sandwiches and daily specials such as crab au gratin at moderate prices for lunch plus well-prepared but much higher-priced entrees for dinner.

Continuing south, historic Lexington, the home of Virginia Military Institute and Washington and Lee University, provides the visitor with several historic sites. The Visitors Center at 107 East Washington Street is the starting point for the three self-guided walking tours of the town. Elegant dining in a restored Classical Revival townhouse can be enjoyed at the Willson-Walker House Restaurant on Main Street.

Just a few miles farther is Natural Bridge, one of the seven natural wonders of the world. In about 1750, a youthful George Washington surveyed the ridge and cut his initials into the towering mass of stone. On July 5, 1774, Thomas Jefferson bought the bridge and surrounding 157 acres from King George III of England for twenty shillings and accurately predicted it would "draw the attention of the world." In the same area are the Natural Bridge Wax Museum and the Caverns of Natural Bridge. Each night the Drama of Creation is re-enacted under the Bridge; this depicts the creation of the world taken from the book of Genesis told with colored lights and music. Meals are available at the adjacent Natural Bridge Hotel.

To Get There: Take I-66 to I-81 south to Christiansburg Exit 37. Follow U.S. 460 west to Blacksburg. Take U.S. 460 Bypass (left fork) around Blacksburg to Rt. 700. Follow Rt. 700 for seven miles to the Resort.

For Reservations: Call 1-800-346-3334 or write Mountain Lake Resort, Mountain Lake, Virginia 24136. Moderate with the meals included.

Williamsburg Inn
Williamsburg, Virginia

Every couple deserves at least one weekend at the Williamsburg Inn. For us who live so close to the Williamsburg area, it would be sheer neglect for us not to take part in our history in this most luxurious fashion. The 232-room Colonial resort, which includes the individual Colonial houses, the Inn, the Lodge, and the Motor Inn, received the five-star Mobil award for a country estate with modern amenities. It is well deserved and a stay at the Inn exposes one to the ultimate in gracious southern living. One of the nation's most distinguished hotels, the Williamsburg Inn is renowned for the excellence of its appointments, its superb cuisine, and its attentive service. Heads of state, political and military leaders from throughout the world, and millions of visitors have experienced the Inn's gracious hospitality.

The manicured lawns and gardens, the long circular drive, and the columned 18th-century white structure introduce the visitor to what is to come. Guests enter through the lobby with conversational groups centered around "Williamsburg" floral arrangements. The rooms have all the modern amenities but are beautifully decorated with Colonial antiques and face either the elaborate gardens to the rear or Colonial Williamsburg to the front. Fresh flowers, a bowl of fruit, and of course some Williamsburg peanuts are on the dresser. Terraces that overlook green countrysides complete the picture for a relaxing getaway weekend for two.

If you haven't been to Williamsburg before, you may want to spend the afternoon in the historic area. Strolling the streets with stops at the various craft shops can be most interesting. At the shops, crafts such as barrelmaking, candlemaking, basketmaking, and spinning and weaving are demonstrated by appropriately dressed workers. There is a wig shop, a gunsmith, an apothecary, and a milliner, among others.

The Capitol presents a twenty-minute lecture that is most informative and the building is lined with many fine portraits of the Colonists. The Governor's Palace is an elegant residence with a walnut-paneled entrance hall decorated with guns and swords, a blue and white ballroom, and a wine cellar with a staircase leading to the cupola. The Capitol grounds offer a perfect opportunity for an afternoon stroll through the trees and gardens.

If you have already seen historic Williamsburg, you may want to drive over to Carter's Grove, six miles east of Williamsburg. This is a beautiful James River plantation home whose original owners, the Carters and the Burwells, occupied powerful positions in Colonial Virginia society. The home shows evidence of the different owners each with different ideas for renovation and consequently no consistent theme in the interior.

Nearby, the quaint riverside village of Yorktown, site of the siege which broke the back of British forces in America, has been restored in piecemeal fashion; modern and historic march side by side. A Victory Center features three different facets of history: events leading up to the Colonists' union and their revolt from British rule; a section displaying portraits, furniture, letters, and other artifacts of the American Revolution; and a third depicting the major events leading to the British surrender at Yorktown. The Yorktown Battlefield and Yorktown National Park offer films and displays as well as pleasant places for walking.

Dinner is going to be a difficult choice. There are many places to choose from. You can't go wrong if you choose the Inn. Dinner at the Inn is an unforgettable experience. The tables are beautifully set, baskets of flowers are everywhere, the wine steward is knowledgeable, the candlelight and piano music are romantic, and the food is superb.

Three restored taverns in historic Williamsburg are currently serving food to the public. The food at Christiana Campbells on Waller Street far exceeds the other two. Christiana Campbells is furnished with original eighteenth-century antiques and reproductions in the simplified style typical of the late 1700's. There are corner cupboards, authentic maps of the period, much decorative pewter, and the tableware is patterned from a design made in mid-eighteenth-century England. The food is "colonial," delicious, and reasonably priced. You may dine inside the tavern, or in good weather, in a small garden towards the rear.

The Trellis, recently opened in Merchants' Square by two area wine connoisseurs, has become recognized as one of the finest restaurants in Virginia. The ambiance is enhanced with gracefully hanging baskets and the food is nouvelle French. Nick's Seafood Pavilion, a short distance east in Yorktown, is the place to go for seafood and is known for its outstanding salad bar. Before retiring, you may want to have a hot toddy in front of one of the Inn's blazing fireplaces or, in summer, simply sit on the lawn admiring the stars.

For Sunday brunch, head for the Cascades Restaurant at the Motor House. Every Sunday, the Lodge provides a buffet that is outstanding and could do well for breakfast, lunch, and dinner. The dining room is most attractive with tall windows overlooking the gardens and a small waterfall.

On your way home, don't miss the Pottery Factory, five miles west of Williamsburg. Covering 138 acres in assorted buildings filled with "bargains," it is a sight in itself. Also on Highway 60 is The Outlet Ltd. Mall offering brand-name merchandise including Dansk, Totes, Manhattan, Burlington, Bass, Aigner, Calvin Klein, Sassoon and Jordache. Or you may want to spend the day in the Old Country at Busch Gardens, located five miles east of Williamsburg.

To Get There: Take I-95 south to Richmond. Head east on Rt. 64 to Williamsburg and follow the signs to the historical area and the Inn.

For Reservations: Call toll free 800-582-8976. Expensive but worth it.

Boar's Head Inn
Charlottesville, Virginia

In the foothills of the Blue Ridge Mountains, The Boar's Head Inn is really more of a resort than a country inn. The hotel contains 175 guest rooms and suites built around an old grist mill, twelve meeting rooms, a ballroom, three dining rooms, and a Sports Club with extensive facilities. The guest rooms are well appointed, many with custom-built furniture, chestnut paneling, and working fireplaces. Each guest room looks out onto gently rolling valleys, lakes, and the ever changing seasonal landscape.

Sports facilities at the Inn include three indoor grasstex courts, ten clay courts and four all weather courts, three squash courts, platform tennis courts, and a Club with health gym and clinic, exercise rooms, saunas, and an adjacent jogging trail. In addition, there is fishing in the lake, swimming in two pools, and even hot air balloon flights to top it all off.

The three dining rooms at the Inn vary from casual to country-gracious. Guests may also choose to enjoy lunch or dinner at the Sports Club. In the hotel, continental food is featured with candlelight and fireplaces. The Tavern, with comfortable leather chairs and wood paneling, is the setting for live entertainment before and after dinner.

Since the hotel is located in Charlottesville, there are many other places to dine. If you are strolling around the University, go across University Avenue from the Rotunda to a commercial strip called "The Corner." This is a collection of burger and T-shirt shops but has several delightful places to eat.

For refined German food, try the Mozart Restaurant on 2nd Street. Quiet elegance sets the scene for wiener-schnitzel, goulash, and duck served with delicacy and finesse. The dining rooms are graced with fresh flowers and the music is Mozart, of course. Alternatively, Bull Alley on West Main Street is a two-tiered dining experience in a converted grocery store. American regional dishes include a crab bisque, fresh salmon steak, and escalope of veal all with locally grown herbs. Downstairs is casual for lunch while upstairs dining is more formal.

In downtown Charlottesville you can have a burger and salad at the Hardware Store Restaurant, a converted emporium in the city's shopping mall, or try fresh pasta at Fellini's, a cozy Italian cafe. One of the most deceiving restaurants is C & O, located on Water Street. It is hidden in a boarded-up building with only a Pepsi sign to indicate its presence. When you step inside, go up the stairs; the. decor is pristine, the cuisine superbly French, and the service is excellent. The Galerie is an outstanding restaurant a short, picturesque drive about eight miles west of town. Especially recommended are the rack of lamb for two, all the seafood dishes, the daily specials and the souffle that must be ordered at the beginning of the meal. Reservations are a must at this top-rated restaurant.

Near Monticello is Michie Tavern, where Thomas Jefferson and James Monroe often met for a drink and to discuss the affairs of the nation. Michie has been run as a tavern since the 1700's. The tavern and outbuildings are interesting and worth a tour. the food is served cafeteria style from 11:30 to 3:00 daily and is said to be the same type the tavern offered 200 years ago—blackeyed peas, stewed tomatoes, green bean salad, cornbread, cole slaw, potato salad, and, of course, southern fried chicken.

Monticello, Ash Lawn, and the University of Virginia are obvious attractions in Charlottesville. No one can fail to be impressed by Jefferson's unique design of Monticello. He selected the Ash Lawn site for his friend. Ash Lawn is a modest farmhouse in contrast to Monticello, but has a spectacular view and boxwood gardens heavily populated with peacocks. A visit to Charlottesville is not complete without a walk around the University, mainly the Jefferson-designed Rotunda and the adjoining Lawn with individual student rooms, the most famous student having been Edgar Allan Poe.

For a recreational break, consider a day on the James River. The James River Runners (804-286-2338) is a tube and canoe outfitter located on the east bank of the James at Hatton Ferry near Scottsville, about a 25-minute drive south from Charlottesville on scenic Route 20. The outfitter drives you upriver about three miles and you drift back with the current in an inflated tube. (Don't forget your bathing suit!) Reservations are recommended as this is a popular activity on a warm summer weekend.

To Get There: Take Rt. 29 south to Charlottesville.

For Reservations: Call 804-296-2181 or write Boar's Head Inn, Box 5185, Charlottesville, Virginia 22905. Expensive but worth it.

HEADING

WEST . . . . .

The Conyers House
Sperryville, Virginia

This will be a memorable getaway weekend for two for two reasons: the quaintness of the Conyers House and the absolutely unequaled dining experience at the Inn at Little Washington.

In 1979, the Cartwright-Browns bought this 1770 house to restore as a country bed and breakfast inn. The present living room was known as Conyers Old Store in 1815 and at Fins' General Store in 1850. The new part of the house was added in 1810; plumbing was added in 1979. Although there are fireplaces throughout, the Conyers House has recently put in central heat and air conditioning. You may select to stay in The Cellar Kitchen or the Church Spring House which are always cool. There are eight rooms to choose from—each different, three with private bathrooms. Among these are "Grampie's Room" with south and east windows, working fireplace, queen-sized four-poster and other antiques; Uncle Sim Wright's room with high ceilings, working fireplace, semi-private bath; and the Hill House, thirty pace uphill from the Main House, with a bed, exposed beams, full bathroom, sitting area, fireplace, jacuzzi and private porch with a mountain view.

While in Sperryville, visit the Faith Mountain Herb Shop for a medley of crafts and gifs, a large selection of herb plantings, and a real old-fashioned flavor.

In 1749, George Washington surveyed the town of Little Washington and today the population barely exceeds its 18th-century number. The streets are laid out exactly as surveyed and are very enjoyable to walk through in every season. There are many historical buildings and interesting shops such as the Country Heritage Antiques and Crafts, and The Village Cafe (a good place for lunch), and the Washington House of Reproductions.

The Inn at Little Washington, about six miles from the Conyers House, is by far the most outstanding dining experience the author can remember. The Inn itself has been through a major restoration and is just elegant. Enormous arrangements of fresh flowers are centered on beautiful antique chests and impeccably appointed tables. The food is nouvelle French and is beyond compare. Don't neglect the homemade soups. At least three different kinds of homemade breads and rolls, piping hot with herbed butter, are served with a salad of herbs and lettuce fresh from the gardens. For an entree, it is hard to beat the chicken with snails, veal with pesto sauce or salmon encroute. The white chocolate mousse or fresh raspberries with cream are perfect endings to exquisite dining. Allow enough time for a drink before or after dinner on the adjacent patio with its attractive plantings and waterfall. The Inn has also recently added a limited number of overnight guestrooms. Although an hour from the Beltway, The Inn at Little Washington is continuously booked. Be sure to call early for reservations.

Back at The Conyers House, a hearty breakfast, included with the price of the room, is served in front of a crackling fire or out on the veranda in warm weather. There are three seatings; sign up on the list on the refrigerator. The house specialty is cheese strata and red pepper jelly served on an English muffin with cream cheese. Also, local cider and delicious parsnip cake are served in the afternoon when you arrive. For those who do not want to pay the prices of the Inn at Little Washington, The Conyers House has recently been offering a four-course, very reasonably-priced dinner in their candlelit dining room.

The Conyers House is just five minutes from Old Rag Mountain, a famous Washington area mountain hiking place.

To Get There: Take Rt. 66 west from the Washington Beltway, exit on Rt. 29 south at Gainesville to Warrenton. Turn west on Rt. 211 and go past Little Washington to Sperryville. Continue through Sperryville on Rt. 522, take a right on Rt. 231 for eight miles. Take a left on Rt. 707 for about a half mile.

For Reservations: Call 703-987-8025 or write at State Mills Road, Sperryville, VA 22740. Moderate.

Red Fox Tavern
Middleburg, Virginia

Here is a place close to home with plenty of atmosphere.
Located in the middle of the Virginia hunt country, forty-
five minutes from D.C., the Red Fox Tavern was built in
1728 by a first cousin of George Washington. The six guest
rooms have been charmingly furnished in the 18th-century
style. Each of the centrally air-conditioned bedrooms has a
four-postered bed with canopy, and a private bath; some
have fireplaces. This is one of several inns in Virginia that
claim to be the "oldest colonial inn." The Inn also offers
thirteen guest rooms in The Stray Fox Inn and McConnell
House, reached through a rear garden walkway and decorated in a similar fashion with braided rugs, quilts and
ruffled curtains.

Hearty country breakfasts, pleasant lunches (try the crab cakes), and gracious candlelight dinners are served in an English pub atmosphere, with cocktails and dining on the terrace in appropriate weather. The Inn makes its own breads, desserts, sauces and soups. Around the corner is the Night Fox Pub featuring a light menu, cocktails, and, occasionally, live music beside the fireplaces.

The main street of Middleburg has several unique boutiques, a country store, many antique shops, and shops for outfitting the "horse set." The Hunt Country sponsors several events throughout the year such as the Steeple Chase and a carriage drive in the spring, the Pony Show in June, and a Wine Festival in autumn. Three especially interesting stores are The Great American Salvage Company, a warehouse of architectural antiques such as mantelpieces, bathtubs and light fixtures salvaged from demolished buildings; The Copper Cricket carrying Laura Ashley home furnishings and handcrafted gifts imported from England; and the Diana Richards Gallery Shop providing a selection of 19th-century English watercolors and engravings.

Virginia is now producing its own wines and the most celebrated of the vineyards is Meredyth, located in Middleburg. Meredyth's Syval Blanc was served in 1976 by President and Mrs. Carter at the White House to the governors of the fifty states. A short and scenic drive from the Red Fox Inn, the vineyards are open to the public for touring. Visitors may walk through the extensive grape-growing area, have a guided tour of the wine making process, and taste a sample of the current wine at a little shop where bottles of the Vineyard's wines may be purchased. For information on tour hours, call 703-687-6277.

Middleburg is the unofficial capital of Loudoun County and a short distance north is historic Leesburg. Originally called Georgetown in honor of King George II, it was renamed in honor of Thomas Lee. Leesburg takes the visitor through two centuries of American history with authentic buildings of diverse architecture. A free, beautifully illustrated, self-guided walking tour map is available from the Information Center. The Loudoun Museum offers demonstrations of pottery making, weaving, spinning, and quilting. The brick-lined streets abound with antique shops, specialty shops, and a wide variety of restaurants.

Two interesting restaurants in Leesburg are the Green Tree and the Laurel Brigade Inn. The Green Tree is located in the historic district of Leesburg on South King Street and features 18th-century cuisine served by waiters in period costumes. Specialty meals include George Washington's favorite bread, Jefferson's dill dressing, and a hot buttered rum. There is baroque entertainment on the weekends. The Laurel Brigade Inn is located on West Market Street, also in the historic district, and advertises "colonial cookery for gentle palates." The Inn boasts that one of their earliest guests was Lafayette, who was visiting President Monroe's Oak Hill estate just south of Leesburg.

Midway between Leesburg and Middleburg is Oatlands, an 1803 Classical Revival home on 260 acres of pasture land that is often the site of the steeplechases. Left to the National Historic Trust by the Corcoran family, tour guides conduct visitors through the family home. Don't miss the formal terraced gardens that include boxwood mazes, a wide variety of perennials and annuals, a bowling green and a reflecting pool.

To Get There: Take the Washington Beltway to Rt. 50 and head west to Middleburg.

For Reservations: Call 703-687-6301 or write Red Fox Inn, P.O. Box 385, 2 East Washington Street, Middleburg, VA 22117. Expensive.

Skyland Lodge
Skyline Drive, Virginia

This is a weekend in which you may wish to include the children. However, nature trails meandering through the hemlock forests, twinkling lights in the valley, the guitarist in the Tap Room, and breakfast while viewing adjacent mountains make it a special weekend getaway for two.

While one can reach Skyland more directly by Rt. 211 through Warrenton, taking I-66 to Front Royal and driving down the Skyline Drive is a much more leisurely way to begin your weekend escape. Skyline Drive is impressive in summer as an escape from the city heat and in fall with the foliage. There are numerous overlooks along the Drive as well as a restaurant, gift shop, and service station at Thornton Gap, approximately thirty miles south of Front Royal.

Forty-two miles south of Front Royal, Skyland Lodge is at the highest point on the Skyline Drive. Accommodations are moderately priced, rustic-motel style, each with its own balcony overlooking the valley. Several cabins with fireplaces are also available. The dining room is glass walled on three sides for magnificent views of the valley and next mountain ridge. The food is Virginia country-style "home cooking" with trout freshly caught in the nearby mountain streams and southern fried chicken or country ham being the standouts.

You may want to bring a picnic lunch to eat along the Parkway or on the Skyline veranda. Then it is time for one of the best hikes in the East. Head for White Oak Canyon parking, about a half-mile from the Lodge. The trail winds through dark, virgin hemlock forests, across mountain streams cascading over jutting rocks, through open, sunlit areas, and finally reaches a spectacular waterfall. You are sure to see a deer or two scampering through the woods. This is not a difficult hike, offers as much varied scenery as you could want, and is about five miles round trip.

The accommodations are in very rustic cabins or motel-style rooms overlooking the valley. There is no air-conditioning, but it is rarely needed. Number 69 and 70 are suites and have a particularly spectacular view. After a rest in your cabin-motel, enjoy the southern cooking in the dining room, the country-western singer or guitarist in the Tap Room, and the lights in the valley seen from your balcony.

Before leaving the next day, be sure to take the hike up to Stony Man. This nature trail is located less than a half-mile north of the Lodge and culminates in a spectacular view of the valley and surrounding mountains. Along the way are markers designating flora and fauna which coordinate with a guide available at the trail's entrance.

You may want to stop at the nationally famous Luray Caverns before heading home. A well-guided tour of about forty-five minutes takes visitors through many rooms of naturally formed stalagmites and stalactites. The Caverns are located about ten miles west or Skyline Drive down Route 211 at the Thornton Gap entrance. While in Luray you may want to stop at the Mimslyn Inn which serves an inexpensive and most enjoyable Sunday brunch as well as other meals.

Heading home, take Rt. 211 at the Panorama intersection of Skyline Drive through Sperryville, Warrenton, and Gainesville to stop at the roadside stands and pick up some cider, apples, or peaches from local farmers. In Warrenton an outstanding place to dine is Sixty-Seven Waterloo in the historic section. Meals are served in several different small rooms of an old Southern mansion and feature traditional and creative French cooking.

To Get There: Take I-66 to Front Royal, follow signs for Skyline Drive. Head south on the Drive for forty-one miles. The Lodge is open from April to October.

For Reservations: Call 703-999-2211 or write Virgina Skyline Co., Inc., P.O. Box 727, Luray, Virginia 22835. Rooms must be reserved well in advance, especially during the fall foliage season. Very reasonable.

Wayside Inn
Middletown, Virginia

Looking for action and night life? This is not the place!
The Wayside Inn in Middletown, Virginia, just of I-81, is
truly a getaway for two. This is the place to enjoy the
warmth and atmosphere of the 18th century. Relax in front
of your own fire in a bedroom furnished in antiques, in
the wine-cellar atmosphere of the stoned-wall Coachyard
Lounge, or in a rocking chair on the front porch.

The Inn was built in 1797 and in the 1960's was completely restored and furnished by a Washington financier
and antique dealer. Each room is decorated with its own
unique flavor, some with canopied beds and their own.
working fireplaces. The public rooms are like small
museums, adorned with objects d'art, paintings, antique
chests, and tables.

There are several small dining rooms, all serving the
Inn's colonial cooking and featuring such items as spoon
bread, peanut soup, pan-fried chicken, and fresh vegeta-

bles from local gardens. In the winter, a favorite eating area is the Old Slave Kitchen with its crackling fireplace. Breakfast features home-made jellies and muffins with the usual choice of eggs, french toast, and pancakes. Warm apple strudel is often available as well.

While the Wayside Inn is mainly a getaway for a couple to just spend time together talking and relaxing, there are some attractions nearby that you may want to visit. Belle Grove is a working farm built in 1794 during Washington's term as President. It is a property of the National Trust for Historic Preservation and visitors may observe quilting, blacksmithing, weaving, rail splitting and other American folk culture and crafts. A little south is the Strasburg Emporium with over 60,000 square feet devoted to antiques, crafts, auctions, and a country store. A short distance from the Inn is Wayside Wonderland, a 250-acre recreational park nestled in the hills with swimming in a natural lake, hiking, fishing, boating, and even some caverns and a battlefield to tour.

There are two restaurants with excellent food just south of the Wayside Inn off I-81. The Edinburg Mill, built in 1848, offers delicious country cooking. Hot yeast rolls right from the oven, pumpkin muffins, Maryland crab-cakes and a variety of chicken dishes highlight the menu. The tables are set with copies of silverware and glassware from the period; pewter salad plates and quilted table cloths contribute to the authentic atmosphere of the original mill building. An adjoining gift store offers a variety of unique locally handcrafted items. In Strasburg, the Hotel Strasburg offers a pub and dining room in the restored atmosphere of a British country inn.

To Get There: Take I-66 to I-81. Go north on I-81 a very short distance to Middletown—Exit 77.

For Reservations: Call 703-869-1797 or write Wayside Inn, 7783 Main Street, Middletown, Virginia 22645. Moderate.

L'Auberge Provençale
White Post, Virginia

Fifty miles west of Washington, D.C. nestled in the rolling hills and farmlands of Virginia is the classic French
country inn L'Auberge Provencale. Charming accommodations, elegant food, and a bucolic setting make this an
outstanding choice for a quiet weekend for two. The drive
out Rt. 50 past the Middleburg estates and farmlands lined
with stone fences with the approaching mountains in the
background encourages city dwellers to unwind enroute.

Dining is in the main stone house (circa 1753). You may
want to have a drink before dinner on the wide white
porch, complete with swing and rocking chairs, which

overlooks the surrounding countryside. There are three intimate dining rooms; each has a working fireplace and pleasantly spaced tables set with country print cloths highlighted by arrangements of freshly cut flowers. Unobtrusive classical music, authentic period furniture, and an impressive, eclectic art collection provide the background for a superb cuisine francaise. The attentive service and beautiful presentation of the selections further contribute to this exceptional dining experience.

The menu features several fresh seafood entrees as well as duck, veal and beef dishes. All are accompanied by vegetables and a salad with many of the ingredients coming from the inn's own gardens. The complimentary homemade cheese sticks served with your drink, hot rye bread, and a cheese course served before dessert are unexpected additions to this gourmet meal.

The guest rooms are in an adjacent building and tastefully decorated with Victorian furnishings in oak, wicker, and pine. Four-poster beds, hardwood floors, hurricane lamps, and dried flowers enhance the country atmosphere. Each room has its own private bath. In the morning guests are offered an impressive breakfast featuring fresh homemade croissants, local fruits, and the quiche, omelet or egg entrees.

This is a good time to travel the back roads beside the Shenandoah River; visit the village of White Post now included on the National Register of Historic Places and a center for restoration of antique and classic automobiles. It is a short drive to Front Royal and the beginning of Skyline Drive (See Skyland Lodge section) or to Winchester, sight of numerous historical buildings such as Stonewall Jackson's headquarters on Braddock Street, General Sheridan's on Picadilly and George Washington's headquarters and surveying office.

Heading back to Washington, you may want to go via Rt. 7 through Leesburg (see Index) picking up some sandwiches at the Bailwick Wine and Cheese Shop to eat at the Hill High Orchards picnic groves along with their fresh cider. Hill High is a 1700-acre farm with pick-your-own fruits and vegetables. During the strawberry season, wagons take the many visitors to the strawberry fields for this purpose. At the Hill High picnic area, you can purchase fruits, vegetables, and homemade pies and cookies.

To Get There: Take Rt. 50 west through Middleburg. Twenty-two miles past Middleburg, take Rt. 340 south for one mile. The inn is on your right.

For Reservations: Call 703-837-1375 or write at White Post, VA 22663. Expensive but worth it.

The Inn at Narrow Passage
Woodstock, Virginia

The Inn at Narrow Passage began as a log farmhouse in the 1740's and served as a haven for settlers traveling through the "narrow passage," a limestone formation dividing the creek and the Shenandoah River. In the 1800's it was first used as a stagecoach stop and then became the family home of the Stovers, whose daughter entertained Stonewall Jackson when he used the house as his headquarters during the Valley Campaign of 1862. Today with the recent addition of a wing, it is a charming bed-and-breakfast inn overlooking the Shenandoah River, winning high marks as a getaway weekend site with its easy accessibility to scenic hikes, historic sites, and nearby skiing.

The inn has twelve guestrooms, six in the newer addition and six in the older portion; some have fireplaces and canopy beds. The rooms in the older section offer a warm and cozy hideaway for winter evenings with their natural stone walls and wooden beams while the newer section offers lighter, airy accommodations with more modern fixtures; eight of the rooms have private baths. But the real atmosphere of a country inn is felt in the front room with its great stone fireplace where guests gather to sip tea or a local Virginia wine on a wintry afternoon or from a rocking chair on the verandahs overlooking the valleys and the hills on a summer's day.

The Inn's location in the northern Shenandoah Valley offers not only the chance to get away but many activities within easy driving distance. Skyline Drive is just a few miles to the east, as are the Luray, Skyline and Shenandoah caverns. Skiing is available a few miles to the west at both Bryce and Massanutten Resorts. Right across I-81 from the Inn is the Shenandoah Vineyards. The winery and vineyards are open year round and welcome visitors with a tour and a wine tasting. On the crest of Massanutten Mountain, four miles from the town of Woodstock, is a tower offering panoramic views of the Valley, the Blue Ridge Mountains, and the seven bends of the Shenandoah River. Or you may choose to just hike leisurely through the four acres on which the inn is sited.

For visitors who like to combine historic sites with beautiful scenery, New Market is just a few miles south. Thousands of students of the Civil War visit the New Market Battlefield Park each year, the scene of the Civil War battles of General Stonewall Jackson's Valley Campaign. It is a well-preserved, 160-acre park with monuments, a Hall of Valor, a museum, and displays. which depict the entire War. The guided walking tour with magnificent views of the valley and mountain ranges is not to be missed if you are in this area. On the other side of I-81 is the Tuttle & Spice General Store and Village Museum adjacent to the Shenandoah Caverns. There are seven "shops" at the Museum featuring thousands of "old store" items such as china dolls, elixers and potions, grandmothers' corsets and high-button shoes. A gift shop offers a wide range of merchandise for sale.

The Inn at Narrow Passage serves only breakfast but it is one of the highlights of the weekend, since it is served to guests in a small stone-walled dining room that shares the great fireplace with the frontroom of the mainhouse. Nearby are several outstanding restaurants for dinner. The Edinburg Mill, a former grist mill built in 1848, provides country cooking at its best, often in the form of a buffet. The homemade breads, crab cakes and chicken dishes are excellent and the surrounding walls and floors of the original grist mill contribute to a most enjoyable dining experience. The Mill is located in Edinburg, a few minutes down U.S. Highway 11. The Spring House, right in Woodstock, is well known throughout the area for its fine continental dishes. For those wanting to take an early evening drive up to Basye, Bryce Resort offers the Copper Kettle Lounge and Restaurant, which overlooks the slopes; a generous buffet of southern cooking and a la carte ordering from the moderately priced menu are available. The lounge has a lively band on the weekends.

To Get There: Take I-66 or Rt. 55 to Highway 11 (where I-66 meets I-81). Head south a few miles to Woodstock.

For Reservations: Call 703-459-8000 or write The Inn at Narrow Passage, U.S. 11 South, Woodstock, Virginia 22664. Inexpensive.

HEADING

EAST . . . . .

Maryland Inn
Annapolis, Maryland

The Maryland Inn, built in 1762, is a 44-room, all brick, three-story inn located one block from the Annapolis Docks. The Inn, located at the vertex of a triangle of streets leading into Church Circle, has a front porch with rockers, a cozy, welcoming lobby, tall ceilings, and period furniture. The rooms vary, and guests would be wise to inspect the choice of rooms that are available at the time.

Arriving around lunch time, you may want to walk over to the Market House, located at the end of the City Docks, purchase ready-to-eat food, and then go across the street to the wine store for a beverage. You are now ready for a picnic either on the waterside benches where you can watch the activities of the harbor, or if you want more privacy, on the rocks that border the harbor in front of the Naval Academy—a great place for boat watching.

For the afternoon, you will need to determine whether your interests are oriented toward history or water activities. The colonial section of Annapolis, and the U.S. Naval Academy, have been registered as National historic landmarks by the federal government. Historic Annapolis, Inc., a nonprofit historical and preservation society, offers the "Historic Annapolis Walking Tour," which includes more than twenty landmarks in the colonial part of the town and on the Naval Academy grounds. The walking tour begins at the Old Treasury Building, where Compromise and Duke of Gloucester Streets converge.

For those wanting more water-oriented activities, there are a great many to choose from. The 300-passenger "Harbor Queen" leaves from the end of the City Dock several times a day and cruises for a forty-five minute tour of the inner and outer harbors, including the Naval Academy, Severn River, Chesapeake Bay, and the Bay Bridge.

Sailboats may be rented at the Annapolis Sailing School at 601 Sixth Street, Eastport, with lessons available. If you would rather let someone else do the sailing, Captain Gerry Morton takes parties of six or less out for five-hour day sails for around $125.00. His "Mustang" is a traditional ketch built in 1907 with forty-six feet of deck. Call 301-268-2144 for reservations. On Sunday, consider reserving passage on the 100-passenger vessel, "Annapolitan II." The ship has an open roof deck, and enclosed lower deck, and departs the City Dock at 10:00 a.m., crossing the Chesapeake Bay to the quaint waterfront village of St. Michaels, Maryland. A three-hour stop allows passengers to walk through the town or visit the Chesapeake Bay Maritime Museum. The ship is back in Annapolis by 5:00 p.m.

Before dinner, you may want to go over to the Annapolis Hilton, located right on the dock, and have a drink at their outdoor lounge in the midst of all the cabin cruisers. For dinner, there are several good choices. The Annapolis Crab House on Main Street is loud and touristy but serves steamed crabs at moderate prices. The Harbour House, overlooking the city dock, has good seafood, especially the crab dishes, and an excellent salad bar. Also, within a block or two of the Maryland Inn, is McGarvey's Saloon and Oyster Bar. This is real "saloon" atmosphere with a macho-looking wood and brass bar that stretches the length of the front room and plenty of Tiffany lamps. Weather permitting, the place to eat here is the sky-lit and mirrored "courtyard." While a large selection of seafood is offered at McGarvey's, there are better places for seafood in Annapolis and the thing to order here is hamburgers—large, thick, juicy, prime meat served with excellent pickles and potato fries that are large oval slices sauteed in their skins.

The King of France Tavern, in the Maryland Inn, is a splendid way to end the evening. The 18th-century tavern offers excellent jazz and is the original "home" of Charlie Byrd and Herb Ellis, who still appear there regularly.

The Treaty of Paris Restaurant, located in the Inn, has purposely been omitted as a recommendation for dinner, although the food is excellent. It is the place for an absolutely outstanding brunch on Sunday morning. The atmosphere is colonial with fireplaces and displays of open-fire cooking instruments. The Treaty of Paris Restaurant offers a buffet-type brunch that would be hard to equal anyplace. An enormous assortment of hot and cold meats, salads, and mouthwatering desserts are beautifully displayed and are very moderately priced. This brunch is something not to miss. The Maryland Inn is one of a group of inns known as "The Historic Inns of Annapolis." Also included in the group are the Governor Calvert House and the State House Inn.

To Get There: Take Rt. 50 west to the Naval Academy exit at Annapolis. This is West Street, which leads directly to Church Circle.

For Reservations: Call 301-263-2641 or write % Historic Inns of Annapolis, 16 Church Street, Annapolis, MD 21401. Expensive but worth it.

Kemp House Inn
St. Michaels, Maryland

If you like four-poster canopied beds, fireplaces, hurricane lamps, fresh flowers, quilts, down pillows, potpourri, and candlelight, the Kemp House Inn is for you. If you like sailboats, yachts, eating on the waterfront, antiques, old village squares, and Victorian houses, the town of St Michaels is for you.

Built in 1805, the Kemp House Inn is a two-story, white brick building with a picket fence, rocking chairs on the porch, and lanterns in the windows. Located on the Eastern Shore in the small town of St. Michaels, the Inn has six guest rooms; four of the rooms have a wash basin and toilet with a shower down the hall, while the two dormer rooms share a bathroom. This is a real country inn with wooden floors, braided rugs, calico curtains, and baskets of flowers everywhere. Working fireplaces in each room contribute to the cozy atmosphere. Breakfast is served in bed or on a small balcony adjoining the bedrooms.

To start your Eastern Shore getaway weekend for two, get in the nautical mood by breakfasting in the dock area of Annapolis. Pick up some freshly baked cheese danish at the Market House to have with your coffee while watching the boats in the harbor.

St. Michaels is only about forty-five minutes from Annapolis, an hour and a half from the Washington area, yet is truly another world. James Michener chose St. Michaels to stay in while writing his book *Chesapeake*. The main street is just three blocks long and has a variety of shops featuring antiques, nautical gear, straw baskets, and various crafts. The Kemp House Inn sits at one end of town within a short walking distance of the harbor. Park your car at the Inn and walk everywhere—a real treat for D.C. commuters.

Crossing the main street in front of the Inn and heading down one block towards the water, take the first left and you will be in the original town square with 17th-century cottages, Revolutionary War cannons, and the town-crier bell. In another block or so, you will see the harbor filled with power and sailing boats of all types and sizes.

If you're ready for lunch, don't miss eating steamed crabs at the Crab Claw. On the waterfront, the restaurant has a deck in the rear that provides the perfect place for eating crabs, watching the boats come and go, and seeing the fishermen unload the oyster catch of the day. Nearby, a sightseeing boat leaves the dock at 11:00, 1:00 and 3:00 every day for a one and one-half hour tour of the bay area and the estates that line the waterfront.

Before dinner you may want to relax on the front porch of the Inn with some wine and cheese available at the shop diagonally across the street. Also, the Longfellow Restaurant on the harbor, about three blocks from the Inn, offers the perfect place for a before-dinner drink with its high stools on the open-air deck in full view of the boats. Patrons may also dine on the deck or in the garden room. The previously mentioned Crab Claw has an indoor restaurant upstairs with a good selection of seafood dishes. Alternatively, gourmet dining in a very luxurious setting is available at The Inn at Perry Cabin about two miles from the Kemp House Inn. A large, 19th-century mansion located on the harbor, there are several elaborately furnished dining rooms, a gazebo on the lawn for drinks, and even six very expensive guest rooms. If this is your choice for dinner, be sure to make reservations well ahead as the wait can be over an hour on weekends.

The town of Oxford, about fifteen miles south of St. Michaels, is even smaller and less commercialized than St. Michael's but well worth a trip. The way to see Oxford is to rent bicycles at The Mews on Dover Street. You can cover the town in less than two hours, stopping at one of the seven marinas for coffee or a cool drink. While in Oxford, the Robert Morris Inn on the Tred Avon River is an excellent place for Sunday brunch or dinner. The Pier Street Marina at the other end of the town is on the bay and offers outdoor dining on crabs as well as a full menu inside.

Further down the peninsula is Tilghman Island, Maryland, a small fishing village. Harrison's Chesapeake House is well known for its seafood and home-style vegetables and features an outdoor bar with a band on the weekends during the summer season. The Tilghman Inn is another possibility for dining or lodging.

On the way back to Washington, you may want to stop in Easton at the Tidewater Inn for Sunday brunch or dinner. This will offer a definite contrast to the Smithton Inn. A handsome and imposing structure of Federal design, the Inn sits on the corner in the center of the town and takes up almost two blocks, with its 120 guest rooms, seven dining rooms, Conference Center, shops, and lounges.

If you haven't had quite enough of crabs, boats, or water by now, east of Annapolis, just before you reach the Bay Bridge, is the Poseidon Restaurant, another place to enjoy crabs while sitting on an open-air deck overlooking the Miles River Basin.

To Get There: Take the Washington Beltway east to Rt. 50. Follow Rt. 50 to Easton. Take Rt. 33 to St. Michaels.

For Reservations: Call 301-745-2243, or write Kemp House Inn, St. Michaels, Maryland. Very reasonable.

Channel Bass Inn
Chincoteague, Virginia

The Channel Bass Inn is a hundred-year-old charming country farmhouse on the "island of ponies." There are ten guest rooms located on the second and third floors, some decorated with antiques and original art. It is a cozy atmosphere perpetuated by the owners who are very friendly and eager to make their guests feel welcome, (which makes up for the fact that the Inn is not located on the water).

The outstanding feature of the Channel Bass Inn, however, is the cooking. Using local seafoods, the chef/owner prepares a unique cuisine with a strong Mediterranean influence. In 1980 and 1981, Mobil Travel Guide awarded Mr. Hanretta their coveted 4-Star Restaurant Award. The owner/chef is now offering three-day cooking vacations. The classes are limited to six people and tuition includes lodging, meals, and complimentary wines. All classes involve demonstration and full participation.

The Inn is located about five miles from the beach at Chincoteague. This island is nothing like the Ocean City area; it is very natural with a somewhat wild flavor. A causeway takes visitors to Assateague, a 33-mile island, most of which is a national wildlife refuge. There are day-use vacation facilities and an excellent beach here. The island is famous for the wild ponies that were featured in the movie "Misty" and supposedly are survivors of a wrecked Spanish galleon. There is a miniature pony farm in the town where you may see the ponies if you don't happen to see them roaming the island. During the summer months, the Wildlife Refuge sponsors safaris through the area. Also available is a scenic sunset cruise.

The National Aeronautics and Space Administration has a facility located in the area with a tour consisting of a drive by the island's rocket-launching facilities in a caravan led by a guide. Interested visitors should report to Wallops Island Causeway Gate via Route 13, Rt. 175, and Rt. 679. There is also an exhibit area on the main base that is open Monday through Friday.

To Get There: Take Rt. 50 west to Salisbury, Maryland. Take Rt. 13 to Rt. 175 to Chincoteague.

For Reservations: Call 804-336-6148 or write at 100 Church Street, Chincoteague, VA 23336. Moderate to Expensive.

Mainstay Inn
Cape May, New Jersey

This getaway weekend for two is different. You arrive by car ferry and stay in a Victorian village. You can spend your time taking long walks on the beach and strolling the historic streets.

Cape May is America's oldest seaside resort; five presidents including Abraham Lincoln have vacationed here. It is located at the southern tip of the New Jersey shoreline and is accessible from the Washington area by a seventy-minute ferry ride from Lewes, Delaware. You can take your car on the ferry or, better still, leave your car in the parking lot and take your bicycle. The ferry makes four trips daily. Call 302-645-6313 for scheduled ferry times.

The Mainstay Inn, built in 1872 as a gentlemen's gambling club, has been carefully restored by the current owners. No detail has been overlooked, from the lace curtains for the many windows, to the music for the grand piano, to the appropriate hats for the hatrack in the hall.

Each bedroom is somewhat different (this is no Holiday Inn!) with marble-topped dressers, armoires, massive beds, and even chamber pots that roll out on trays from underneath. (Not to worry, the chamber pots are for authenticity only; the rooms have baths.) Those staying in the Inn will feel more like houseguests of the owners than paying customers as they are given the run of the place from the living room to the cupola. There are only eleven rooms available for rent so it is important to reserve early, especially in the summer months.

Cape May was made for walking: walks through the small streets to see the lived-in Victorian houses with wisteria-covered double verandas, cupolas, captain's walks and wicker rockers on the front porches; walks through the historical section along the cracked slate sidewalks under gas lamps; walks through the Victorian "mall" lined with small cafes.

Then there is the beach, several miles long. In midsummer near the center of town, the sand will be spotted with umbrellas and sunbathers; children will be splashing in the cold New Jersey coastline waves. There is even a small boardwalk featuring a penny arcade. As you walk farther down the beach, heading west toward the lighthouse, the crowds thin and the sunbathers are replaced by surfcasting fishermen. There are occasional jetties of huge boulders jutting out to sea. From the end of the third jetty, you can see a mile down the coast line to the lighthouse.

You will want to get back to the Mainstay for afternoon tea served with warm gingerbread on the veranda while you make your decisions for dinner. Near the boardwalk is the Jetty Restaurant, which serves three modestly priced meals a day of seafood fresh from the net. The Lobster House, overlooking the bay, is just outside the town limits and even offers cocktails on an adjacent sloop. If you choose

the Lobster House, go early so you will have time to stroll
along the wharf and watch as the catches of the day are
unloaded. A few miles north of Cape May on Ocean
Drive is Two-Mile Landing offering open-air dining
alongside the waterways, and all-you-can-eat steamed crab
area, and a more formal restaurant featuring fresh seafood
at reasonable prices.

The Mad Batter restaurant is well known in the area for
the high quality offerings of eclectic food. It is owned and
run by Harry Kulkowitz, "retired" from the Bronx. The
daily specials are listed on a blackboard and include French,
Italian, and Jewish dishes at moderate prices. Even breakfast at the Mad Batter is a feast, often including such things
as whole-wheat pancakes with creme anglais. Poisson Fume
Nicoise (local fish smoked and served with a light mustard
sauce), or a seafood crepe. However, rates at the Mainstay
usually include a delicious breakfast served in the dining
room under a beautiful chandelier, or in good weather, on
the veranda.

Cape May night life is very limited; for those who need
more action there is Atlantic City, just an hour's drive up
the coast. See Atlantic City in Index.

To Get There: Take Rt. 50 east to Rt. 404, then Rt. 9 to
Lewes, Delaware, where you take the ferry.

For Reservations: Call 609-884-8690 or write Mainstay Inn,
635 Columbia Avenue, Cape May, New Jersey 08204.
Expensive but worth it.

HEADING

for the

CAPITOL . . . . .

Crystal Gateway Hotel
Arlington, Virginia

It is not necessary to leave the Washington area to have a very special getaway weekend for two. The new Marriott Crystal Gateway Hotel is just the place for relaxing in elegant and beautiful surroundings with plenty of activities available if you are interested. Located in Crystal City, the Hotel is connected by underground passages to the Crystal Underground Shops and Metro system. The lobby of the Hotel is spectacular with its greenhouse atrium, marble stairs, and numerous comfortable conversation areas. The Crystal's Lounge is part of the lobby and offers a lovely place for having a drink and enjoying the piano bar. Some of the rooms have an excellent view of Washington; all are beautifully decorated and equipped.

If you have already "done" Washington, you may want to spend your weekend at the Hotel's indoor-outdoor pool, health club, exercise room, and saunas. Indoor tennis and racquetball are available in the nearby Crystal Underground which also contains over thirty shops and boutiques. The Crystal Dinery, in the Underground, has ethnic stalls offering a large selection of foods that can be eaten in the courtyard.

Alternatively, consider spending the afternoon in Olde Towne Alexandria. Head for Ramsey House, Alexandria's oldest house and the city's Visitor Center at the corner of King and Fairfax Streets. Information on shops, historic buildings, restaurants, and excellent maps for a walking tour are available here from the Tourist Council. Along with visiting the 18th-century houses and noting the varying architecture, be sure to allow some time for the Topedo Factory Art Center on Union Street along the river. Three floors of the recently renovated building have been divided into spaces for artists of all types not only to display their products but to do their work on the premises. Take time to go out the back door of the Art Center and sit on the benches overlooking the Potomac. In good weather, consider renting bicycles at 1114 South Washington Street and cycling down the path along the Mount Vernon Parkway for beautiful scenery along the Potomac.

There are many excellent restaurants in Alexandria to choose from. Bamiyan II, on the corner of King and Fairfax, offers a unique opportunity to try Afghan food at its best; try the fixed-price-dinner which includes several courses and a selection of their specialties. Le Refuge on Washington Street is a warm and authentic auberge-type French restaurant with a variety of delicious entrees that change with the season. Several blocks west of the waterfront, along King Street, is Terrazo, an excellent example of fine northern Italian cooking, as is Geranio a couple of doors up the street. Taverna Cretekow, with its whitewashed walls in the Mediterranean style, Greek crockery and wall hangings is one of the most attractive restaurants in the Washington area; in good weather you may choose to dine in the back garden. Eastwind, on the north side of King Street, offers elegant and creative Vietnamese food in a lovely setting. La Bergerie, on North Lee Street, is often selected as one of Washington's outstanding restaurants; the decor is impressive and the atmosphere upscale but intimate as you enjoy the well-prepared classic French food. Around the corner, on Queen Street, is Bilbo Baggins, a cozy cafe-type restaurant featuring bread freshly baked on the premises, a delicious house salad, and fresh seafood and veal daily specials. The wine bar upstairs offers wine by the glass and imported beer. For more casual dining, try a bowl of "the world's best" clam chowder at the Fish Market or a sandwich from the deli in the Small Mall, both on King Street a block up from the water.

If you have saved touring Alexandria for Sunday, you may want to stop for brunch at Gadsby's Tavern on North Royal Street. The Tavern has been restored to look much as it did in George Washington's time; the fireplace mantels are the original, the staff are dressed in period costumes, and the food is colonial. Other places for brunch in Alexandria are the Holiday Inn on King Street which offers an extensive five-course buffet, Bread and Chocolate, two blocks west, featuring fresh pastries, breads and cheeses, Chadwicks off Union Street and on the water for an a la carte breakfast, and Two-Nineteen, on King Street, serving Creole and low French cuisine in several elaborate dining rooms.

To Get There: Take the Crystal City exit off Rt. 395 (Shirley Highway).

For Reservations: Call 703-920-3230, or write at 1700 Jefferson Davis Highway, Arlington, VA 22202. Moderate with the special weekend rate.

Vista International Hotel
Washington, D.C.

Spectacular! Impressive! First Class! This is guaranteed
to be your reaction when you enter the Vista International
Hotel located a few blocks from The White House in Washington, D.C. From the top-hatted doormen who greet you
as you enter the 14-story skylighted atrium to the tower of
six Givenchy-designed suites that rises in the center of the
lobby, you will know you are in one of our nation's pre-
miere hotels.

The Vista opened in February 1983 and is conveniently
located within easy walking distance of The White House,
the new Convention Center, Connecticut Avenue boutiques, and several of Washington's top-rated restaurants.

It is a short taxi ride to the Smithsonian Museums, George-town, or the Kennedy Center. The Hotel is very elegant and very expensive but offers several different weekend package plans that make it affordable. While the Givenchy suites are not included in the weekend prices, a "Posh and Pampered Weekend" on the Executive Wing is. The Wing is a beautifully decorated area with luxurious accommodations; fresh bouquets of flowers are everywhere. A center lounge for the Executive Wing has its own bar and serves free hors d'oeuvres in the afternoons and danish pastries in the mornings. The package plan includes two nights lodging, dinner and a bottle of wine in the American Harvest Restaurant, Sunday morning champagne brunch, tourmobile tickets for Washington sightseeing, and indoor valet parking. At a much lower rate, there is the "Super-sale" weekend which includes the valet parking and a welcome cocktail and is available for only one night's stay.

In the hotel, along with the elegant Georgetown mansion-style American Harvest Restaurant serving regional American cuisine, there is the more casual Verandah Restaurant overlooking the lobby and serving complete meals as well as wines, cheeses, and desserts. Afternoon tea is served in the Givenchy lounge, a large balcony area adjacent to the suites. The intimate Federal Bar has specialty drinks and live entertainment. A fitness center provides sauna, massage facilities and modern exercise equipment.

There are so many things to do and see in Washington, D.C. that it is difficult to know where to start or what to mention in this book. Details about the many museums of the Smithsonian Institution are available in any hotel or information center. If you have already been to the mall museums, don't miss the Portrait Gallery (the outdoor patio is a lovely place for lunch), the National Museum of African Art, and the Library of Congress located just east of the Capitol.

The Corcoran Gallery of Art and the National Geographic Society are both within walking distance of the Hotel. Located on 17th Street and New York Avenue, the Corcoran Gallery is the largest of the private museums in

Washington. Founded in 1869, the museum concentrates on the display and documentation of American art. It has an extensive collection of American paintings, drawings, prints, sculpture and photography plus frequently changing exhibitions. The museum is open Tuesday through Sunday from 10:00 to 4:30 and Thursday evenings.

The National Geographic Society is at 17th & M Streets. Explorers Hall contains many exhibits relating to National Geographic-sponsored expeditions and research such as Admiral Peary's dog sled used on his polar trip, Cousteau's diving saucer, and an impressive display of photography from around the world. A model of the solar system and the world's largest unmounted globe are interesting exhibits to study. The Hall is open seven days a week.

In general, this section of the book will concentrate on activities in the Georgetown area. For things to do and see or places to eat in Alexandria, see the Index. While Washington's metro system does not go to Georgetown, the area may be easily reached by taxi or the Georgetown Trolley (ask Hotel Concierge).

Georgetown is a place for walking. Begin at the intersection of M Street and Wisconsin Avenue and walk in any direction. Heading north on Wisconsin Avenue, you will pass such shops as the outlet of designer Alexander Julian, the Georgetown University Shop on the corner of 36th Street for classic clothes, the Phoenix with handloomed cotton dresses from Mexico, the Audubon Book Shop, and Little Caledonia—a small gem of a shop with distinctive gift items. If it is lunch time, stop at the American Café for some homemade soup or their unique sandwiches served on the best and freshest croissants in town.

Along M Street, west of the Wisconsin intersection, you will see Georgetown Park on your left. The four-story, Victorian-style mall contains several pleasant restaurants and a mixture of nationally known shops such as FAO Schwartz, Caché, Abercrombie & Fitch, and Liberty of London. Local shops include Les Enfants, Georgetown Zoo, and the Cookbook Store.

Heading South from M Street, you will come upon the C & O Canal, historic in its own way since it was surveyed by George Washington. In the 1800's, this was a commercial enterprise with mules pulling barges on the canal. The mules still pull the barges today working for the National Park Service and taking visitors on leisurely summertime rides. The rides begin on the canal at 30th and Thomas Jefferson Streets each Wednesday through Sunday at 10:30 a.m. and 1 and 3:00 p.m. For more information, call 299-2026. Alternatively you may want to bicycle up the canal along the tow path and stop at the Old Angler's Inn for brunch or a drink. Bicycles can be rented at Fletcher's boathouse along with canoes and rowboats.

If the weather is good, consider a cruise down the Potomac. Washington Boat Lines, Inc. (554-8000) offers cruises from March 31st through Labor Day leaving the Georgetown dock every hour on the halfhour starting at 10:30 a.m. If you are more in the mood for a leisurely nature walk, head for Dumbarton Oaks or Theodore Roosevelt Island. Dumbarton Oaks, where world leaders met in 1944 to organize the United Nations, is at 32nd and R Streets in Georgetown. Today the estate is a Harvard research museum and library dedicated to Byzantine and early Christian Art. Spring through fall, there are no gardens more beautiful than those surrounding the museum.

Theodore Roosevelt Island is in the middle of the Potomac across from Georgetown. It is entered from George Washington Parkway, just east of Key Bridge. A mile-long path circles the island which has been kept in a natural state. You will go through a forest of oak, maple, elm, dogwood and cypress trees; border a swamp, a marsh and lowlands; and end up in the center of the park at the monument to Theodore Roosevelt. Farther away are Rock Creek Park with designated nature trails and Great Falls Park with waterfalls cascading into the Potomac.

Washington has become a restaurant town with every nationality represented along with some fine American cuisine. Before dinner, there are two especially nice places for having a drink. In Georgetown, the Georgetown Inn

offers half-price drinks, free appetizers and an excellent
pianist. All this can be enjoyed in front of a large picture
window overlooking the hustle and bustle on Wisconsin
Avenue. The Hotel Washington, within walking distance
of the Vista, offers an excellent view of The White House
and other monuments from its roof-top terrace.

Maison Blanche and Dominique's are two very elegant
and quite expensive French restaurants near the White
House and the Vista Hotel. Both offer a fixed-price, pre-
theater dinner that is reasonable and outstanding both in
quality and variety of selections. Dominique's was the win-
ner of the 1983 Travel/Holiday Award as an outstanding
restaurant in America. It is noted for exotic dishes such as
rattlesnake meat, buffalo and ostrich, along with the more
expected fare.

Two very reasonably priced ethnic restaurants are located
near the Hotel: Iron Gate Inn and Gusti's. The Iron Gate
Inn continues to be voted the best cafe and most romantic
restaurant by readers of "Washingtonian Magazine." The
restaurant is a converted 19th-century horse stable.
Wooden beams, a stone fireplace, and candlelight contribute to a very pleasant and intimate atmosphere. In the
summer, there is a tranquil garden for outdoor dining .
Gusti's is a large Italian restaurant with ten separate dining
areas, each with a distinctive mood, as well as an outdoor
cafe for sidewalk dining in the summer.

Georgetown is the place for ethnic restaurants of every
type. The Apana and the Tandoor are moderately priced,
award winning Indian restaurants, both located on M Street.
Between these two is El Caribe, featuring food from South
America and Spain along with Latin American entertainment. Candelas is a northern Italian Restaurant, quite
expensive, but of very high quality and with a romantic
atmosphere. On Wisconsin Avenue is Old Europe, a German restaurant specializing in schnitzel and seasonal
Bavarian dishes in a setting of German paintings and other
objects d'art. It is consistantly rated among the top restaurants in the Washington area. Farther down Wisconsin is
Serbian Crown, an intimate, smartly appointed establish-

ment serving fine Russian Serbian cuisine. Very expensive, it is considered to be one of the best restaurants in the area. The crystal chandeliers and authentic paintings of Balkan legends contribute to a really unique dining experience, as do the 28 varieties of frozen Vodkas that are offered.

The Kennedy Center has brought theater and music to the Washington area that competes with New York and Philadelphia. With its avenue of flags and the bronze bust of John F. Kennedy, the marble edifice on the banks of the Potomac is impressive just to walk through. The Center is comprised of three major performance areas: the Eisenhower Theater is used for plays, film screenings and one-man shows; the Concert Hall is for visiting orchestras, jazz concerts, and the National Symphony performances; the Opera House is the home of the American Ballet Theater. Arena Stage, Folger Theatre, and Ford's Theatre offer additional contributions to the cultural scene with first-rate, professional plays.

In Georgetown there are cafes and pubs offering entertainment on every corner. Tucked away down by the C & O Canal is Blues Alley, a mecca for jazz buffs from around the country. A carriage house for the fire department over two hundred years ago, the club was converted from a garage in 1965. Brick walls and dim lighting give a sense of intimacy. Entertainment starts at 9 p.m. and often includes some of the top names in traditional and contemporary jazz. Other places with live entertainment are The Fish Market, Deja Vu, Aster Restaurant, The Saloon, and Poseurs.

A recent addition to the Georgetown scene is Washington Harbor, a architecturally eclectic collection of offices, condominiums, stores and restaurants on the river next to the Whitehurst Freeway. Take some time to sit on the benches and watch the boats, walk around and inspect the realistic sculptures by a member of the Johnson & Johnson family, and enjoy the fountain before dining in one of several good restaurants. Tony and Joe's is a highly rated and reasonably priced informal seafood restaurant with an outdoor patio for dining in good weather. Hisago and Jaimalito's are excellent upscale Japanese and Mexican restaurants, respectively.

During the summer, there are many special events in the downtown Washington area. Among them: free concerts on the steps of the Capitol and the Jefferson Memorial by bands from the Armed Services and occasionally the National Symphony; jazz, folk, blues, and pops concerts on the C & O Canal; the Marine Parade including the Silent Drill Team and the Drum and Bugle Corps at the Marine Barracks; and A Shakespeare Festival on the grounds of the Washington Monument. Ask the Hotel Concierge for more information on these events.

For Reservations: Call 202-429-1700 or write Vista International Hotel, 1400 M Street, N.W., Washington, D.C. 20005. Moderate to expensive with the special weekend rate.

INDEX

102

INDEX OF RESTAURANTS

NOTES

NOTES

NOTES

NOTES

About the Author

June Harrington Marquis lives in Alexandria, Virginia. She has a bachelor's degree in mathematics and a masters degree in educational psychology. June has been an elementary school teacher, high school mathematics teacher, and a mathematics specialist for Fairfax County Public Schools, Fairfax, Virginia. Currently she is on leave to teach at George Mason University in Fairfax. Her husband, Dennis, is a scientist with the Government. They have four girls, one of whom was the illustrator for this book. For many years, June and Dennis have taken getaway weekends for two, always finding it time and money well spent.